# REVELATIONS
## OF DIVINE LOVE

# REVELATIONS
## OF DIVINE LOVE

Julian of Norwich

*With an Introduction by*
DOM ROGER HUDLESTON
(Monk of Downside Abbey)

DOVER PUBLICATIONS, INC.
Mineola, New York

*Bibliographical Note*

This Dover edition, first published in 2006, is an unabridged republication of the 1952 (second) printing of the work first published in 1927 by Burns, Oates and Washbourne, Ltd., London, under the title *Revelations of Divine Love, Shewed to a Devout Ankress by Name Julian of Norwich* (edited from the MSS. by Dom Roger Hudleston, O.S.B., Monk of Downside Abbey).

*International Standard Book Number*

*ISBN-13: 978-0-486-45244-9*
*ISBN-10: 0-486-45244-1*

Manufactured in the United States by LSC Communications
45244105     2018
www.doverpublications.com

# INTRODUCTION

## I. THE MANUSCRIPTS

FOUR MSS. of the *Revelations of Divine Love* are known to exist: three in the British Museum, and one in the Bibliothèque Nationale at Paris. In order of antiquity they rank as follows:

(1) Brit. Mus., MSS. Additional, No. 37790, dated 1413, purchased from Lord Amherst's library in 1909, and described in the Catalogue of Additional MSS., 1906–1909. There seems no doubt that this is the MS. described in Blomefield's *History of Norfolk* (iv. 81), as being in the possession of the Rev. Francis Peck (1692–1743), but subsequently lost sight of until the dispersal of the Amherst library. This MS. consists of a series of medieval devotional works, and the version of the *Revelations*—which is very much shorter than that given in the other MSS.—is introduced by a Preface which runs as follows. "Here es a vision schewed be the goodenes of God to a deuoute Woman and hir name es Julyan that is recluse atte Norwyche and yitt ys on lyfe. Anno dno millmoCCCCxiii. In the whilke Vision er fulle many comfortabylle wordes and gretly styrrande to alle thaye that desyres to be crystes looverse." At the end is a colophon: *"Explicit Juliane de Norwych."*

(2) Bibl. Nationale, Paris, Fonds Anglais, No. 40 (Bibliotheca Bigotiana 388). This is a sixteenth-century MS., without title-page: of its origin nothing is known. As, however, it appears to be the original from which Dom Serenus Cressy published his printed version (issued *sine loco* in 1670), it may *perhaps* have belonged to the convent of Benedictine nuns at Paris, to whom Cressy acted as Chaplain during the years 1651–3, but this is purely conjectural.

It has a colophon: "*Explicit liber Revelationum Julyane ana-torite* [*sic*] *Norwyche cuius anime propicietur Deus.*"

(3) Brit. Mus., MSS. Sloane, No. 2499, seventeenth century. This MS. does not mention the author of the *Revelations* by name. Of its origin, or how it came into the Sloane collection, there is no record. It is divided into sections, with chapter headings added by the transcriber.

(4) Brit. Mus., MSS. Sloane, No. 3705. This is a MS. of the early eighteenth century, possibly copied from No. 3 above, but considerably modernized in spelling and language. In some passages, however, there are readings peculiar to itself, and the scribe has added the following colophon: "Here end the Sublime & wonderful Revelations of the unutterable Love of God in Jesus Xt, vouchsafed to a dear Lover of His, and in her to all His dear friends & Lovers, whose hearts, like hers, do flame in the Love of our Dearest Jesu."

Besides these four MSS. there was one formerly in the possession of Pierre Poiret, author of a *Catalogus Auctorum Mysticorum* (Amsterdam, 1702), the existence of which is vouched for by Tersteegen in the Preface to his *Auserlesene Beschreibungen Heiliger Seelen*; the whereabouts of this MS., if it still exist, is unknown.

## II. PRINTED EDITIONS

(1) *XVI Revelations of Divine Love*, Shewed to a Devout Servant of our Lord, called "Mother Juliana," an Anchorete of Norwich: Who lived in the Dayes of King Edward the Third. Published by R. F. S. Cressy. *Accedite ad Deum et Illuminamini*, Psal. 33 v. 5. Printed in the Year MDCLXX. *Permissu Superiorum*. This is the edition referred to above as based on the Paris MS. It was reprinted under the editorship of G. H. Parker (Leicester, 1843), and again, with a Preface

by the Rev. George Tyrrell, S.J. (London 1902, 2nd edition 1920).

(2) *Revelations of Divine Love*, shewed to a devout Anchoress, by name Mother Julian of Norwich. With a Preface by Henry Collins (London, 1877). This edition is based upon MS. Sloane 2499, but with modern spelling, the text also being modernized very considerably. It soon went out of print and was never reissued.

(3) *Revelations of Divine Love*, Recorded by Julian, Anchoress at Norwich, *Anno Domini* 1373. *In lumine tuo videbimus lumen*. A version from the MS. in the British Museum, edited by Grace Warrack (London, 1901). This edition also is based upon MS. Sloane 2499, in modern spelling; but the text has been kept much nearer to the MS. than in the edition of Father Collins. It has a long Introduction by Miss Warrack and an excellent Glossary, and has been reprinted eight times between 1901 and 1923.

(4) *The Shewings of the Lady Julian*, Recluse at Norwich, 1373. (Previously entitled "Comfortable Words for Christ's Lovers.") Transcribed and edited from the earliest known MS. (Brit. Mus. Addit. 37790) by the Rev. Dundas Harford, M.A., Rector of Scunthorpe, Norfolk (London, 1925). (N.B. The title given above is that of the third edition, the two earlier editions, bearing the title *Comfortable Words*, etc., were issued in 1911 and 1912.) This edition is based upon the Amherst MS. (No. 1 *supra*), and is of special interest as giving the shorter version, which the editor, Rev. Dundas Harford, holds to be the original or "first edition" of the *Revelations*. This textual problem is discussed *infra* (Introduction, No. IV).

Besides the above, the following should be mentioned:

(5) *Mystiques Anglais. Révélations de l'amour divin* à Julienne de Norwich, Recluse de XIV^e siècle. Traduites par Dom G. Meunier, Moine Bénédictin (Paris, 1910, 2nd edition,

1925). This translation has an interesting Introduction and some useful Notes by Dom Meunier.

In the present edition the text has been based upon MS. Sloane 2499, of which a full and careful collation has been made. While adopting modern spelling throughout, the actual wording of the text has been kept considerably closer to that of the MS. than in the editions of Miss Warrack or Father Collins, although really obsolete words have been abandoned in favour of the nearest modern equivalent. Some readers may perhaps regret that this process has not been carried further: but the experience gained in preparing other volumes of the *Orchard Books* has convinced the editor that readers of these medieval English works of devotion get accustomed to such minor archaisms as have been retained so easily that the slight extra effort demanded thereby is more than compensated for by the gain to the reader in retaining the actual wording and the flavour of the original. I gladly take this opportunity of acknowledging my indebtedness to Miss Warrack's admirable edition of the work, although I have differed from her in my reading of certain passages of the MS., which, despite its comparatively recent date, is difficult to decipher in a good many places. I have also printed the chapter headings—which appear in this MS. only, and are presumably the work of the transcriber—with some curtailment, however, especially after Chap. 50, when they tend to become inordinately long. A few Notes on difficult passages, and a Glossary of archaic words, changed or retained, have been added at the end. Throughout the book words added to make the meaning clearer have been placed within square brackets.

### III. THE AUTHOR

Of the Author of this work nothing is known save what she herself relates in her *Revelations*, and what the scribe who copied the earliest MS. of them tells us about her.

By putting together the details thus obtained we learn that her name was Julian, and that she was a Recluse or "Ankress" who lived in a cell attached to the Church of St Julian at Norwich. The foundations of this cell may still be seen, on the south side of the chancel of St Julian's, with the Squint, or low side window, through which she was accustomed to hear Mass.

The Revelations, she tells us, were shewed to her "in the year of our Lord 1373, the eighth day of May" (Chap. 2), when she was "thirty years old and a half" (Chap. 3), which gives the date of her birth as somewhere in the latter half of 1342: and as the scribe of the Amherst MS. tells us that she was "yet on life *anno domini* 1413", she must have lived to be over seventy years old. The statement in Blomefield's *Norfolk* (IV. 81) that she was a hundred years old is due to an error by which he read MCCCCxlij instead of MCCCCxiij, when quoting from the MS. in question.

The same MS. gives us the interesting detail that her mother was present on the occasion of the Revelations,[1] but nothing is known of her family or position in life, beyond her own description of herself as "a simple creature that could no letter". Since, however, she entered upon the life of an ankress while still quite young, it is more than likely that her family was comparatively well to do, as the cost of her support and of a servant to attend upon her would presumably be borne by her relatives.

The fact that the Church of St Julian belonged to the Benedictine nunnery of Carrow has led to the suggestion

[1] *The Shewings of Lady Julian*, p. 59; *vide infra*, Note 2, p. 171.

that Julian herself was a Benedictine: but there is no evidence that this was so, unless the fact that she once quotes the *Life of St Benedict*, which forms Book II of the *Dialogues* of St Gregory, be held to support the theory, which, moreover, it would be difficult to reconcile with her illiteracy.

On this latter point, however, it would be wrong to insist too strongly, since her book reveals a mind by no means uninstructed, but rather one that has penetrated deeply into the mysteries of the Catholic religion, both on its doctrinal and its personal sides, and it would not be difficult to produce parallel cases of holy souls in whom the grace of God has more than made up by illumination for the lack of ordinary education.

To judge from her book, Julian would seem to have been a very spiritual, devout soul, deeply sensitive to the beauty of holiness, and centred wholeheartedly upon the love and service of God: while, for the age in which she lived, her consecration of herself as an ankress would excite nothing of the wonder it would arouse to-day. Indeed, if we may argue from the small number of manuscripts of her *Revelations*, and from the total absence of contemporary references to her, she must have attracted but little notice, and was probably unknown beyond her immediate neighbourhood.[1] But that fact—however much we may regret it—would undoubtedly have been accepted by Julian herself as a special favour of God and a sign of his approval.

### IV. PROBLEM OF THE TWO TEXTS

The reappearance of the Amherst MS., which gives a text of the *Revelations* containing only about a quarter of the matter in the later MSS., has raised a textual problem of no small difficulty.

At first sight one might be inclined to dismiss the shorter

[1] But see the postscript, p. xxvii.

text as being merely a series of extracts from the complete work: and the fact that the MS. in question contains a number of such extracts from medieval devotional works would seem to support such a conclusion. A closer examination, however, shows that the shorter text not only differs in its wording from the longer one in a great many passages, but that it also gives a certain number of details which are entirely wanting in the longer version.

As a result of his careful study and comparison of the two texts, the Rev. Dundas Harford, who has edited the shorter version (*v. supra*, p. vii), gives it as his opinion that the Amherst text "is what might be called the 'first edition' of the *Revelations*", while the longer text "is the outcome of the twenty years' subsequent meditation, thought, and experience, referred to in the fifty-first and in the last chapters of the later version".[1] The present editor, while at first disinclined to accept this theory, has now, after many months of work upon this edition, come round to the view that Mr Harford is most probably right.

This leaves us, however, in the unsatisfactory position of having no manuscript of the entire work earlier than the Paris codex, which belongs to the sixteenth century—two hundred years or so later than the date of the actual Revelations on 8 May 1373—though both the Paris MS. and Sloane 2499 appear to derive from a fourteenth-century original, the spelling and dialect of which they have retained. This lost archetype seems to have been written in a mixed East Anglian and Northern dialect, and, of the two copies, Sloane 2499 is perhaps nearer to the original text. Unless, therefore, the lost fourteenth-century original of the longer version is found, we are not likely to obtain a better text of this than appears in Sloane 2499, which has accordingly been used as the basis of the present edition.

Assuming that Mr Harford's theory is correct, there re-

[1] *The Shewings of Lady Julian*, p. 8.

mains the further problem why the scribe of the Amherst MS.—who wrote in 1413, forty years after the date of the Shewings, and who was able to vouch for the fact that Julian was still alive—should have preferred to give the first and shorter account of the Revelations rather than the fuller one, which was presumably in existence at the date in question, seeing that the most important of the additions is definitely stated to have been given "twenty years save three months after the original vision" (v. infra, Chap. 51). This question, however, must remain unanswered.


## V. CIRCUMSTANCES OF THE REVELATIONS

The *Revelations of Divine Love* were shewn to Julian on 8 May 1373, which was the third Sunday after Easter, but she tells us that some time before that date she had desired "three gifts of God. The First was mind of his Passion; the Second was bodily sickness in youth, at thirty years of age; the Third was to have of God's gift three wounds . . . that is to say, the wound of very contrition, the wound of kind compassion, and the wound of wilful longing toward God" (Chap. 2). She says further that she had asked the two first desires "with a condition", viz. if such were God's will: the last, however, she asked "without any condition". She mentions also that the first two desires passed from her mind, but that the third one dwelled with her continually.

When she was thirty and a half years old, a sickness such as she had desired came upon her and lasted for a week, during which she received the last Sacraments, and on the seventh day "her body was dead from the middle downwards," she was unable to speak, and her curate, or parish priest, was sent for. He came and held the crucifix before her, after which her sight began to fail and it was all dark about her, "save on the Image of the Cross", whereon she

beheld "a common light", but "wist not how". After this the
upper part of her body began to die and she "weened soothly
to have passed. And in this [moment] all pain was taken
from me, and I was as whole . . . as ever I was afore"
(Chap. 3).

She seems to have passed into a state wherein bodily consciousness almost ceased; not, however, her mental activi-
ty, for she "marvelled at this sudden change, for methought
it was a privy working of God, and not of kind [i.e., not
natural]. Then came suddenly to my mind that I should
desire the second wound," viz. "that my body might be filled
with mind and feeling of his blessed Passion . . . but in this
I desired never bodily sight nor shewing of God [i.e., no
vision], but compassion, such as a kind soul might have with
our Lord Jesus . . . and therefore I desired to suffer with
him."

Then suddenly, as if in answer to her wish, the figure on
the crucifix seemed to come to life. "I saw the red blood
trickling down under the Garland," or crown of thorns,
"hot and freshly and right plenteously, as it were in the time
of his Passion": and this sight of the head of Christ crucified
seems to have remained present to her during the Revelations or "Ghostly Shewings" which followed.

The first fifteen of the Shewings followed continuously
during the course of some five hours. "The first began early
in the morn, about the hour of four, and they lasted, shewing by process full fair and steadily, each following other,
till it was nine of the day overpassed" (Chap. 65).

During all this time Julian seems to have remained without consciousness of pain, at any rate so far as her body was
concerned, for "I had no grief nor dis-ease as long as the
Fifteen Shewings lasted following: and at the end all was
close and I saw no more . . . and anon my sickness came
again: first in my head with a sound and a din, and suddenly

all my body was full-filled with sickness, like as it was afore. And I was as barren and dry as [if] I had never had comfort but little. And as a wretch I moaned and cried, for feeling of my bodily pains, and for failing of comfort ghostly and bodily" (Chap. 66).

At this return of suffering she seems to have lost faith for a little while in the truth and genuineness of the Revelations, and before proceeding to describe the Sixteenth Shewing she feels it incumbent on her to acknowledge her failure. "First me behoveth to tell you as anent my feebleness, weakness, and blindness," for she accounted this afterwards as "a great sin, great unkindness, that I, for folly of feeling of a little bodily pain, so unwisely lost for a time the comfort of all this blessed Shewing," and she adds, "here may you see what I am of myself" (Chap. 66).

This self-accusation and confession of her loss of faith is, to my mind, a detail of great importance, since it shows how disinclined Julian was to self-deception. Indeed, not only does her whole narrative ring true, but, by a number of small touches, she reveals that the natural tendency of her mind was sceptical rather than credulous: a trait of character which is of great value when we remember that her book, in its final form, represents the outcome of twenty years' meditation upon the Revelations that were crowded into a few hours only.

She explains clearly how she came to be convinced that the Shewings were genuine and her short-lived doubt about them a delusion, for—after describing the loss of faith just referred to—she adds: "But herein would our courteous Lord not leave me. And I lay still till night, trusting in his mercy, and then I began to sleep." While thus sleeping she saw, or dreamed that she saw, the devil, who made an assault upon her, as if to strangle her. "This ugly shewing was made sleeping, and so was none other. But . . . our courteous Lord gave me grace to waken: and scarcely had I my life." Then follows a very curious detail, which seems to show that the incident could not have been a dream merely. "Anon a light smoke came in the door, with a great heat and a foul stench. I said, '*Benedicite, Domine!* it is all on fire that is here!' I asked them that were with me if they felt any stench. They said, Nay: they felt none. I said, 'Blessed be God' . . . and anon all vanished away, and I was brought to great rest and peace, without sickness of body or dread of conscience" (Chap. 66).

With this cessation of suffering her faith in the genuineness of the Revelations returned, and that night the Sixteenth Shewing was made to her, when "our Lord opened my ghostly eye and shewed me my Soul in the midst of my heart. I saw the Soul so large as it were an endless world, and as it were a blissful kingdom. And by the conditions that I saw therein I understood that it is a worshipful city. In the midst of that city sitteth our Lord Jesus, God and Man, a fair Person of large stature, highest Bishop, solemnest King, most worshipful Lord; and I saw him clad solemnly. And worshipfully he sitteth in the Soul, even-right in peace and rest. And . . . the place that Jesus taketh in our Soul he shall never remove it, without end, as to my sight: for in us is his homeliest home and his endless dwelling" (Chap. 67). "And he gave me to know soothfastly that it was he that shewed me all afore . . . and soon after all was close, and I saw no more" (Chap. 68).

Although it would seem that Julian never again experienced anything parallel to the Visions, these served her as a basis for contemplation for many years to come, during which "in ghostly shewing" she received further light from God, whereby she was able to understand more fully and express more clearly what had been revealed to her in the Sixteen Revelations.

## VI. NATURE OF THE VISIONS

Since the time of St Augustine theologians have agreed in dividing visions into three classes—Corporeal, Imaginative, and Intellectual—according to the analysis given by him in *De Genesi ad literam*, XII, vii.

In Corporeal visions—with which may be coupled locutions and any other supernatural manifestations which are, or appear to be, perceived by means of the senses—either a figure really present externally strikes the retina or other organ of sense, and there determines the physical phenomena of the vision: or else an agent superior to man directly modifies the eye, or other sensual organ, so as to produce a sensation equivalent to that which an external object would produce.

An Imaginative vision is the sensible representation of an object by the action of the imagination alone, without the aid of the eye or other sensual organ. In such visions the subject may be aware that the object apparently seen exists only in his imagination, or he may, so to speak, project it without himself, in which case there is hallucination. Mystical writers note that Imaginative visions usually last for a short time only; either (1) because if the subject attempt to define or fix the elements of the vision by conscious effort he tends to destroy it altogether, or (2) because they soon give place to Intellectual visions.

Intellectual visions are those in which no sensible image is perceived, but the intelligence is enlightened directly, without the aid either of images, external or imagined, or even of the reasoning faculty. St Teresa describes this type of vision thus: "We see nothing, either interiorly or exteriorly . . . but without seeing anything the soul conceives the object and feels whence it is, more clearly than if it saw it, save that nothing in particular is shewn to it. It is like feeling someone near one in a dark place" (First Letter to Fr Rodrigo Alvarez). These Intellectual visions are, naturally, those which mystics find it most difficult to describe. Sometimes, indeed, they are admittedly incapable of being expressed in human language, in which case they are said to be ineffable (*cf.* 2 Cor. xii. 4).

In Julian's case all three types of communication were experienced, and she herself distinguishes them quite clearly. "All this was shewed by three ways: that is to say, by bodily sight, and by word formed in mine understanding, and by ghostly sight. But the ghostly sight I cannot nor may not shew it as openly nor as fully as I would. But I trust in our Lord God Almighty that he shall of his goodness, and for your love, make you to take it more ghostly and more sweetly that I can or may tell it" (Chap. 9).

As will be seen later, in the analysis of the Visions given in Section VII of this Introduction, Julian's Corporeal visions were mostly connected with the Passion of Christ: as at the outset of all, when "suddenly I saw the red blood trickling down from under the Garland, hot and freshly and right plenteously, as it were in the time of his Passion, when the Garland of thorns was pressed on his blessed head . . . I conceived truly and mightily that it was he himself shewed it to me without any mean" (Chap. 4).

A little further on in the same chapter she says: "He brought our blessed Lady to my understanding. I saw her ghostly, in bodily likeness . . . also God shewed in part the wisdom and the truth of her soul." This clearly was an Imaginative vision.

From these lower forms she passes to purely Intellectual vision: "In this same time our Lord shewed me a ghostly sight of his homely loving . . . also our Lord God shewed that it is full great pleasance to him that a silly soul come to him nakedly and plainly and homely" (Chap. 5); or again:

"In this an inward ghostly Shewing of the Lord's meaning descended into my soul" (Chap. 51).

Julian's experience follows the general rule also in this, that, while the Corporeal and Imaginative visions were apparently limited to the one great occasion on the eighth day of May and the night following, her Intellectual visions or illuminations occurred at intervals during many years after that—e.g., "fifteen years after, and more, I was answered in ghostly understanding" (Chap. 86); and again: "Twenty years after the time of the [fourteenth] Shewing, save three months, I had teaching inwardly" (Chap. 51).

While on this subject, mention must be made again of the highly interesting passage quoted above, in which Julian herself puts on record her personal conviction of the reality of the Shewings, and notes especially her inability to record in words all that she experienced in the purely Intellectual visions. "All this was shewed by three ways: that is to say, by bodily sight, and by word formed in mine understanding, and by ghostly sight. But the ghostly sight I cannot nor may not show it as openly nor as fully as I would" (Chap. 9).

It is impossible in the space here available to deal with the question of visions and their nature as fully as the subject invites, but mention must be made of two details in which Julian's experience differed from that of the majority of mystics. The first of these is the interesting and unusual feature that, during her visions, Julian appears to have remained conscious, in part at any rate, of what was going on around her: "For this sight I laughed mightily, and that made them to laugh that were about me, and their laughing was a liking to me" (Chap. 13). The second, that, while she was experiencing the special assault of the Evil One (during the period of doubt or loss of faith which occurred between the fifteenth and sixteenth Shewings) she was uncertain whether or no the fire and stench which accompanied it were objective, and so consulted the bystanders about it: "I asked them that were with me if they felt any stench. They said, Nay: they felt none. I said 'Blessed be God!' For that I wist well it was the Fiend that was come to tempest me" (Chap. 66). This eminently practical way of solving her doubt upon the matter is characteristic of Julian's humility and strong common sense.

## VII. ANALYSIS OF THE REVELATIONS

The *Revelations of Divine Love* is not a difficult work to follow, but it may be a help to the reader to give here a short analysis of the Sixteen Shewings, so that he may follow more easily the sequence of ideas which runs through them: for one of the great features of the work, and one which gives it a very peculiar interest, is the way in which the visions progress and lead the soul onwards to a very striking concept of its own relations to God, a concept which, one cannot doubt, represents simply the state of mind and heart to which Julian herself attained.

In the first Revelation (Chaps. 4–9), she was shewn the Trinity, and perceived, through the sufferings of Christ, the goodness and love of God for all that he had created: "He shewed me a little thing, the quantity of a hazel-nut . . . and I thought, 'What may this be?' And it was generally answered thus, 'It is all that is made.' I marvelled how it might last, for methought it might suddenly have fallen to naught for littleness. And I was answered in my understanding: 'It lasteth, and ever shall [last] for that God loveth it.' And so all thing hath the Being by the love of God" (Chap. 5).

The second Revelation (Chap. 10), which deals with the fall of man, his redemption, and the necessity for co-operation on man's part, leads on to the third (Chap. 11), in which Julian is shewn how all Being is of God and is good, while sin is no Being. This chapter, which begins with the words, "And after this I saw God in a Point"—a phrase remarkable both for its neo-Platonic flavour and for its parallelism to Dante—shows that, although Julian "could no letter", her intellect was quite capable of grasping and meditating upon some of the deepest problems of philosophy.

In Revelations four to seven (Chaps. 12–15), Julian is shewn how the stain of sin is washed away by "the dear-worthy blood of our Lord Jesus" (Chap. 12): and that so effectually, that all the evil which God suffereth Satan to do "is turned for us to joy, and for him to shame and woe" (Chap. 13): while the labours of the creature in co-operating with God's grace—albeit done solely by means of the strength received from him—are rewarded in heaven with three degrees of bliss (Chap. 14): although, in this life, man is often left by God with "no comfort nor none ease . . . but faith, hope, and charity" (Chap. 15), as a test of his perseverance, not as a result of sin.

The eighth Revelation, which occupies the whole of Chaps. 16 to 21, deals with the sufferings of Christ in his Passion, and the spiritual martyrdom of our Blessed Lady and of all lovers of Christ through compassion. Herein Julian was shewn how all men, as members of Christ's mystical body, "be now . . . in his Cross with him, in our pains and our Passion, dying . . . and the cause why he suffereth [it to be so] is for that he will of his goodness make us the higher with him in his bliss, and for this little pain that we suffer here, we shall have an endless, high knowing in God, which we might never have without that" (Chap. 21).

The ninth Revelation (Chaps. 22 and 23), which shews forth the joy of Christ in that he suffered his Passion for love of man, and tells how the soul of man may share in his joy, leads up to the tenth (Chap. 24), wherein the soul, through the wound of love, enters into the heart of Christ.

The Revelations now cease to be connected directly with the Passion, and the eleventh and twelfth (Chaps. 25 and 26), which are concerned with the blessed Mother of Jesus and with God as Sovereign Being, lead up to the very long thirteenth Revelation, which occupies no less than fourteen chapters (Chaps. 27–40).

This Shewing—with which Chaps. 44–63 are intimately connected—deals with the existence of evil and of sin, problems which have troubled many minds, and none more than the mystics', whose whole view of life tends to look upon unity and goodness as the underlying essentials of creation. In Julian's case her childlike submission to the Church's teaching, and the practical good sense which is so marked an element of her character, prevent her from shirking the difficulty or from denying its reality as some minds do.

First of all Julian clears the ground, so far as actual pain and suffering are concerned, by regarding these simply as opportunities for union with God by compassion. This treatment of the problem is typical of the mystics, those familiar friends of God, who are on such terms of intimacy with him that, to them, the joy of union seems cheaply purchased at the price of any pain: much in the way that the joy of human friendship, manifested in sympathy, is felt to be a distinct gain due to the suffering which occasions it. Julian realizes fully how such an outlook makes for union, and states her view in the striking phrase: "I saw that each kind compassion that man hath on his even-Christians with charity, it is Christ in him" (Chap. 28).

The fundamental problem, why God should ever have permitted sin, had already occupied her for long, and was to do so for many years still. "Methought: 'If sin had not been, we should all have been clean and like to our Lord, as he made us.' And thus, in my folly, afore this time often

I wondered why by the great foreseeing wisdom of God the beginning of sin was not letted: for then, methought, all should have been well. . . But Jesus, who in this Vision informed me of all that me needeth, answered by this word and said: 'It behoved that there should be sin; but all shall be well, and all shall be well, and all manner of thing shall be well' " (Chap. 27).

This promise of Christ Julian accepted in all simplicity; the trouble was, how to reconcile it with the Church's teaching as to the effects of sin on the soul. She knew, of course, and understood the ordinary Scholastic doctrine, that evil and sin have no substantive existence, but are simply the negation of good: "I saw not sin, for I believe it hath no manner of substance nor no part of being, nor could it be known but by the pain it is cause of" (Chap. 27). But this teaching by itself failed to satisfy her, and she asked again: " 'Ah! good Lord, how might all be well, for the great hurt that is come, by sin, to thy creatures?' . . . And to this our blessed Lord answered . . . that Adam's sin was the most harm that ever was done, or ever shall be, to the world's end. . . Furthermore he taught that I should behold the glorious satisfaction" which he—Christ—had made for that sin: adding, "since I have made well the most harm, then it is my will that thou know thereby that I shall make well all that is less" (Chap. 29).

There remained still the question of eternal punishment in hell, which it seemed impossible to reconcile with the promise that "All manner of thing shall be well": and Julian has her own way of dealing with it. "Our Faith is grounded in God's word, and it belongeth to our Faith that we believe that God's word shall be saved in all things; and one point of our Faith is that many creatures shall be damned: as angels that fell out of heaven for pride, which be now fiends; and man in earth that dieth out of the Faith of Holy Church, that is to say, they that be heathen men; and also man that hath received christendom and liveth unchristian life and so dieth out of charity: all these shall be damned to hell without end, as Holy Church teacheth me to believe. And all this [so] standing, methought it was impossible that all manner of things should be well, as our Lord shewed in this time. And as to this I had no other answer in Shewing of our Lord God but this: 'That which is impossible to thee is not impossible to me: I shall save my word in all things and I shall make all things well.' This I was taught, by the grace of God, that I should steadfastly hold me in the Faith as I had aforehand understood, [and] therewith that I should firmly believe that all things shall be well, as our Lord shewed in the same time. For this is the Great Deed that our Lord shall do, in which Deed he shall save his word in all thing and he shall make all well that is not well. How it shall be done there is no creature beneath Christ that wotteth it, nor shall wit it till it is done; according to the understanding that I took of our Lord's meaning in this time" (Chap. 32).

There remains a point of her teaching with regard to sin that is extremely difficult to understand, the more so because she is less clear than usual in dealing with it. This is her view that, in the souls of the predestined, there is a supreme point which never sins. "God brought to my mind that I should sin . . . and therein I conceived a soft dread. And to this our Lord answered: 'I keep thee full surely.' This word was said with more love and secureness and ghostly keeping than I can or may tell. For as it was shewed that I should sin, right so was the comfort shewed: secureness and keeping for all mine even-Christians. . . For in every soul that shall be saved is a Godly Will that never assented to sin, nor ever shall. Right as there is a beastly will in the lower part that may will no good, right so there is a Godly Will in the higher part, which will is so good that it may never will ill, but ever good. And therefore we are that which he loveth, and endlessly we do that which him pleaseth. This shewed our Lord in [shewing] the wholeness of love that we stand in, in his sight: yea, that he loveth us now as well while we are here, as he shall do while we are there afore his blessed face. But for failing of love on our part, therefore is all our travail" (Chap. 37).[1]

As it stands this passage cannot be reconciled with Catholic theology, but perhaps the explanation is that Julian has produced a certain confusion by trying to combine two theological truths: first, the Immutability of God's love for us, since in him *there is no change, nor shadow of alteration*,[2] so that, however much we sin, we cannot make him love us less—or, as Julian herself puts it in Chap. 61, "We shall verily see in heaven, without end, that we have grievously sinned in this life, and notwithstanding this, we shall see that we were never hurt in his love, nor were never the less of price in his sight"; and secondly, the truth that the elect of God are those *Blessed . . . to whom the Lord hath not imputed sin*,[3] on which passage St Bernard does not hesitate to write: "It is enough for me for all justification to have him only propitious against whom I have sinned. For all that he has decreed not to impute to me is as though it had not been,"[4] a passage the memory of which may not impossibly have inspired Julian to speak as she does.

Another passage, which seems to bear out this interpretation of Julian's words, occurs in Chap. 40, where she tries to provide against the danger of her language being misunderstood: "If any man or woman, because of all this ghostly comfort that is aforesaid, be stirred by folly to say

---

[1] Also Chap. 53.    [2] James i. 17.    [3] Rom. iv. 8.
[4] St Bern., *in Cant. Serm.*, xxiii. 15. See Note 4, p. 174, for the whole passage.

or think: 'If this be sooth, then were it good to sin [so as]
to have the more meed'—or else to charge the less [guilt]
to sin—beware of this stirring: for soothly if it come it is
untrue, and of the enemy of that same love that teacheth us
all this comfort." Still, when all allowances have been made,
it must be admitted that the words in Chap. 37 go too far,
and are liable to mislead a reader who is unskilled in theology.

The fourteenth Revelation occupies Chaps. 41–43, and
is concerned with Prayer: after which there follows the
long section already referred to (Chaps. 44–63), which
develops still further Julian's teaching with regard to sin.

Then in Chaps. 64 and 65, we have the fifteenth Revelation, in which Julian—abandoning all her anxieties about
sin and evil—pours out her soul in burning words on what
is, for her, the supreme Shewing of all, viz. the love of
God for man's soul, and the supreme joy of union with him,
so that "thou shalt never more have pain: no manner of sickness, no manner of misliking, no wanting of will: but ever
bliss and joy without end" (Chap. 64); for "the Charity of
God maketh in us such a unity that, when it is truly seen, no
man can part himself from other" (Chap. 65).

Chap. 66 describes the incident of her temporary loss of
faith in the Revelations, referred to above; after which
interlude comes the sixteenth and last of the Shewings
(Chaps. 67 and 68), wherein she perceived the indwelling
of God in the soul. "I saw the Soul so large as it were an
endless world, and . . . I understood that it is a worshipful
City. In the midst of that City sitteth our Lord Jesus, God
and Man, a fair Person of large stature, highest Bishop,
solemnest King, most worshipful Lord; and I saw him clad
solemnly. And worshipfully he sitteth in the Soul, even-
right in peace and rest . . . and the place that Jesus taketh
in our Soul he shall never remove it, without end, as to my

sight: for in us is his homeliest home and his endless dwelling" (Chap. 67). After this followed a last assault of the Evil One, which "occupied me all that night, and on the morn till it was about prime day" (Chap. 69).

The remaining chapters (Chaps 70–86) consist chiefly of considerations upon and explanations of the Sixteen Shewings, in which Julian elaborates the meaning of her visions in the light of her meditation and contemplation during many years. These chapters are full of deep spiritual insight, expressed in words of unrivalled beauty, and they give a wonderful picture of her soul. The final passage of the whole may well be quoted here, as the conclusion of all that she had learned in her long life of utter self-abandonment and search after God, when—the wheel having come full circle—she finds herself back at the point from which she set out upon her mystic journey, the eternal mystery of the Love of God.

"From that time that it was shewed I desired oftentimes to witten what was our Lord's meaning. And fifteen years after, and more, I was answered in ghostly understanding, saying thus: 'Wouldst thou witten thy Lord's meaning in this thing? Wit it well: Love was his meaning.

" 'Who shewed it thee? Love.

" 'What shewed he thee? Love.

" 'Wherefore shewed it he? For Love.

" 'Hold thee therein and thou shalt witten and know more in the same. But thou shalt never know nor witten therein other thing without end.' Thus was I learned that Love was our Lord's meaning.

"And I saw full surely in this and in all, that ere God made us he loved us; which love was never slacked nor ever shall be. And in this love he hath done all his works; and in this love he hath made all things profitable to us; and in this love our life is everlasting. In our making we had beginning;

but the love wherein he made us was in him from without beginning: in which love we have our beginning. And all this shall we see in God, without end. Which may Jesus grant us. Amen."

G. ROGER HUDLESTON, O.S.B.

St Wulstan's,
Little Malvern.
18 *October* 1926.

## POSTSCRIPT

[In the year 1934 was discovered the long-lost autobiography of a contemporary of Dame Julian's, viz. Margery Kempe, of King's Lynn in the same county of Norfolk. The manuscript is considered to be a copy, made about the year 1450, of an original written in the period 1436–8. In her eighteenth chapter Margery Kempe tells of a visit which she made to the city of Norwich and of her intercourse during that visit with Dame Julian. The date of the meeting is not given, but it may be set down approximately as lying between 1400 and 1410. A transcript of Margery Kempe's account of the conversations between these two very different persons is subjoined, this transcript being taken from the edition of her book which has been published by the Early English Text Society (Original Series, No. 212). The spelling is modernized and a few obsolete words are given their modern equivalents. Here is Margery's account.

"And then she was bidden by Our Lord for to go to an ankress in the same city which hight Dame Jelyan. And so she did and showed her the grace that God put in her soul of compunction, contrition, sweetness and devotion, compassion with holy meditation and high contemplation, and full many holy speeches and dalliance that Our Lord spake to her soul, and many wonderful revelations, which she showed to the ankress to learn if there were any deceit in them, for the ankress was expert in such things and good counsel could give. The ankress, hearing the marvellous goodness of Our Lord, highly thanked God with all her heart for his visitation, counselling this creature to be obedient to the will of Our Lord God and fulfil with all her mights whatever he put in her soul, if it were not against the worship of God and profit of her even-Christians; for, if it were, then it were not the moving of a good spirit but rather of an evil spirit. The Holy Ghost moveth never a thing against charity; and, if he did, he were contrarious to his own self, for he is all charity. Also he moveth a soul to all chasteness, for chaste livers be called the temple of the Holy Ghost; and the Holy Ghost maketh a soul stable and steadfast in the right faith and the right belief. And a double man in soul is ever unstable and unsteadfast in all his ways. He that is evermore doubting is like to the flood of the sea, the which is moved and borne about with the wind, and that man is not like to receive the gifts of God. What creature hath these tokens, he must steadfastly believe that the Holy Ghost dwelleth in his soul. And much more, when God visiteth a creature with tears of contrition, devotion, or compassion, he may and ought to believe that the Holy Ghost is in his soul. Saint Paul saith that the Holy Ghost asketh for us with mournings and weepings unspeakable, that is to say, he maketh us to ask and pray with mournings and weepings so plenteously that the tears may not be numbered. There may none evil spirit give these tokens, for Jerome saith that tears torment more the devil than do the pains of hell. God and the devil be evermore contrarious, and they shall never dwell together in one place; and the devil hath no power in a man's soul. Holy Writ saith that the soul of a rightful man is the seat of God; and so, I trust, sister, that ye be. I pray God grant you perseverance. Set all your trust in God and fear not the language of the world; for the more despite, shame, and reproof that ye have in the world, the more is your merit in the sight of God. Patience is necessary unto you, for in that shall ye keep your soul. Much was the dalliance that the ankress and this creature had by communing in the love of Our Lord Jesus Christ many days that they were together."]

# CONTENTS

# CONTENTS

CONTENTS

## CONTENTS

# CONTENTS

## CONTENTS

# REVELATIONS
# OF DIVINE LOVE

REVELATIONS TO ONE WHO COULD NOT
READ A LETTER, ANNO DÑI, 1373

## THE FIRST CHAPTER

### Of the number of the Revelations particularly

THIS is a Revelation of Love that Jesus Christ, our
endless bliss, made in Sixteen Shewings, or Revelations particular.

Of the which the First is of his precious crowning with
thorns; and therewith was comprehended and specified the
Trinity with the Incarnation, and unity betwixt God and
man's soul; with many fair shewings of endless wisdom and
teachings of love: in which all the Shewings that follow be
grounded and oned.[1]

The Second is the discolouring of his fair face in token of
his dearworthy[2] Passion.

The Third is that our Lord God, Almighty Wisdom, All-
Love, right as verily as he hath made everything that is, also
verily he doeth and worketh all-thing that is done.

The Fourth is the scourging of his tender body, with
plenteous shedding of his blood.

The Fifth is that the Fiend is overcome by the precious
Passion of Christ.

The Sixth is the worshipful thanking of our Lord God

[1] i.e., made one, united.    [2] i.e., honoured.

I

in which he rewardeth his blessed servants in Heaven.

The Seventh is often feeling of weal and woe—feeling of weal is gracious touching and lightening, with true sickerness of endless joy, the feeling of woe is temptation by heaviness and irksomeness of our fleshly living—with ghostly understanding that we are kept also sickerly in Love, in woe as in weal, by the Goodness of God.

The Eighth is the last pains of Christ, and his cruel dying.

The Ninth is of the liking which is in the Blissful Trinity of the hard Passion of Christ and his rueful dying: in which joy and liking he will[eth that] we be solaced and mirthed with him, till when we come to the fulhead in Heaven.

The Tenth is, our Lord Jesus sheweth in love his blissful heart even cloven in two, rejoicing.[1]

The Eleventh is an high ghostly Shewing of his dearworthy Mother.

The Twelfth is that our Lord is most worthy Being.

The Thirteenth is that our Lord God will[eth] we have great regard to all the deeds that he hath done: in the great nobleness of all things making, and of the excellency of man's making, which is above all his works; and of the precious amends[2] that he hath made for man's sin, turning all our blame into endless worship.[3] Where also our Lord saith: "Behold and see! For by the same Mighty Wisdom and Goodness I shall make well all that is not well; and thou shalt see it." And in this he will[eth] that we keep us in the Faith and truth of Holy Church, not willing to know his secrets[4] now, but as it [be]longeth to us in this life.

The Fourteenth is that our Lord is the Ground of our Prayer.[5] Herein were seen two properties: the one is rightful prayer, the other is secure trust; which he will[eth

---

[1] MS. "enjoyand".      [2] MS. "Asseth", i.e., making satisfaction.
[3] i.e., honour, glory.      [4] MS. "to wit his privities".
[5] MS. "beseekeing".

should] both be alike large; and thus our prayer pleaseth[1] him and he of his Goodness fulfilleth it.

The Fifteenth [is] that we shall suddenly be taken from all our pain and from all our woe, and of his Goodness we shall come up above, where we shall have our Lord Jesus to our meed and be fulfilled of joy and bliss in Heaven.

The Sixteenth is that the Blissful Trinity, our Maker, in Christ Jesus our Saviour, endlessly dwelleth in our soul, worshipfully ruling, and giving us all things mightily, and wisely saving and keeping for love; and we shall not be overcome of our Enemy.

## THE SECOND CHAPTER

### Of the time of these Revelations, and how she asked three petitions

THESE Revelations were shewed to a simple creature that could no letter the year of our Lord 1373, the eighth day of May. Which creature desired afore three gifts of God. The First was mind of his Passion; the Second was bodily sickness in youth, at thirty years of age; the Third was to have of God's gift three wounds.

As in the First, methought I had some feeling in the Passion of Christ, but yet I desired more by the grace of God. Methought I would have been that time with Mary Magdalene, and with other that were Christ's lovers, and therefore I desired a bodily sight wherein I might have more knowledge of the bodily pains of our Saviour and of the compassion of our Lady and of all his true lovers that [had] seen, that time, his pains. For I would be one of them and suffer with him. Other sight nor shewing of God desired I

[1] MS. "liketh".

3

never none, till the soul were departed from the body. The cause of this petition was that after the shewing I should have the more true mind in the Passion of Christ.

The Second came to my mind with contrition; [I] freely desiring that sickness [to be] so hard as to death, that I might in that sickness receive all my rites of Holy Church, myself weening that I should die, and that all creatures might suppose the same that [had] seen me: for I would have no manner comfort of earthly life. In this sickness I desired to have all manner [of] pains bodily and ghostly that I should have if I should die, with all the dreads and tempests of the fiends, except the outpassing of the soul. And this I meant[1] for [that] I would be purged, by the mercy of God, and after live more to the worship of God because of that sickness. And that for the more speed in my death: for I desired to be soon with my God.

These two desires, of the Passion and the sickness, I desired with a condition, saying thus: "Lord, thou wottest what I would—if it be thy will that I have it—; and if it be not thy will, good Lord, be not displeased: for I will naught but as thou wilt."

For the Third [gift], by the grace of God and teaching of Holy Church I conceived a mighty desire to receive three wounds in my life: that is to say, the wound of very contrition, the wound of kind[2] compassion, and the wound of wilful[3] longing toward God.[4] And all this last petition I asked without any condition.

These two desires aforesaid passed from my mind, but the third dwelled with me continually.

[1] i.e., desired.     [2] i.e., natural.     [3] i.e., earnest, with set will.
[4] See Note 1, *infra*, p. 171.

## THE THIRD CHAPTER

### Of the sickness obtained of God by petition

AND when I was thirty years old and a half, God sent me a bodily sickness, in which I lay three days and three nights; and on the fourth night I took all my rites of Holy Church, and weened not to have lived till day. And after this I lingered on[1] two days and two nights, and on the third night I weened often-times to have passed;[2] and so weened they that were with me.

And being in youth as yet, I thought it great sorrow to die—but for nothing that was in earth that meliked to live for, nor for no pain that I was afeared of—for I trusted in God of his mercy. But it was to have lived that I might have loved God better and longer time, that I might have the more knowing and loving of God in bliss of Heaven. For methought all the time that I had lived here—so little and so short in regard[3] of that endless bliss—I thought [it] nothing. Wherefore I thought: "Good Lord, may my living-no-longer be to thy worship!"[4] And I understood by my reason and by my feeling of my pains that I should die; and I assented fully with all the will of my heart to be at God's will.

Thus I [en-]dured till day, and by then my body was dead from the middle downwards, as to my feeling. Then was I minded to be set upright, under-leaning with help,—for to have more freedom of my heart to be at God's will, and thinking on God while my life would last.

My Curate was sent for to be at my ending, and by when[5]

---

[1] MS. "I langorid forth".　　　[2] i.e., I thought often that I was dying.

[3] MS. "reward".

[4] Or, as in Cressy's version: "May my living be no longer to thy worship?"

[5] MS. "then".

he came I had set my eyes, and might[1] not speak. He set the Cross before my face and said: "I have brought thee the Image of thy Maker and Saviour; look thereupon and comfort thee therewith."

Methought I was well [as I was], for my eyes were set uprightward into Heaven, where I trusted to come by the mercy of God; but nevertheless I assented to set my eyes on the face of the Crucifix, if I might[1]; and so I did. For methought I might longer dure to look evenforth[2] than right up.

After this my sight began to fail, and it was all dark about me in the chamber, as if it had been night, save in the Image of the Cross whereon I beheld a common light; and I wist not how. All that was beside the Cross was ugly to me, as if it had been mickle occupied with the fiends.

After this the other part of my body began to die, so far forth that scarcely I had any feeling;—with shortness of breath.[3] And then I weened soothly to have passed.

And in this [moment] suddenly all my pain was taken from me, and I was as whole (and specially in the other part of my body) as ever I was afore.

I marvelled at this sudden change; for methought it was a privy working of God, and not of nature.[4] And yet by the feeling of this ease I trusted never the more to live; nor was the feeling of this ease any full ease to me: for methought I had liefer have been delivered from this world.

Then came suddenly to my mind that I should desire the second wound of our Lord's gracious gift: that my body might be fulfilled with mind and feeling of his blessed Passion. For I would that his pains were my pains, with compassion and afterward longing to God. But in this I desired never bodily sight nor shewing of God, but compassion

[1] i.e., could.    [2] i.e., straight before me.    [3] MS. "wind".
[4] MS. "kind".

[such] as a kind[1] soul might have with our Lord Jesus, that for love would be a mortal[2] man: and therefore I desired to suffer with him.

## THE FOURTH CHAPTER

### Here beginneth the First Revelation of the precious crowning of Christ

IN this suddenly I saw the red blood trickling down from under the Garland hot and freshly and right plenteously, as it were in the time of his Passion when the Garland of thorns was pressed on his blessed head [that was] both God and Man, the same that suffered thus for me. I conceived truly and mightily that it was himself shewed it me, without any mean.[3]

And in the same Shewing suddenly the Trinity fulfilled my heart most of joy. And so, I understood, it shall be in heaven without end to all that shall come there. For the Trinity is God: God is the Trinity; the Trinity is our Maker and Keeper, the Trinity is our everlasting lover, everlasting joy and bliss, by our Lord Jesus Christ. And this was shewed in the First [Shewing] and in all: for where Jesus appeareth, the blessed Trinity is understood, as to my sight.

And I said: "Benedicite, Domine!" This I said for reverence in my meaning, with a mighty voice; and full greatly was astonied for wonder and marvel that I had, that he, that is so reverend and dreadful, will be so homely with a sinful creature living in wretched flesh.

This I took for the time of my temptation,—for methought by the sufferance of God I should be tempted of

[1] MS. "kinde", i.e., true to its nature.    [2] MS. "deadly".
[3] i.e., intermediary.

fiends ere I died. With this sight of the blessed Passion, with
the Godhead that I saw in mine understanding, I knew well
that it was strength enough for me, yea, and for all creatures
living, against all the fiends of hell and ghostly temptation.

In this he brought our blessed Lady to my understanding.
I saw her ghostly, in bodily likeness: a simple maid and a
meek, young of age and little waxen above a child, in the
stature that she was when she conceived with child. Also
God shewed in part the wisdom and the truth of her soul:
wherein I understood the reverent beholding that she beheld her God and Maker [with], marvelling with great
reverence that he would be born of her that was a simple
creature of his making. And this wisdom and truth—knowing the greatness of her Maker and the littleness of herself
that was made,—caused her to say full meekly to Gabriel:
"Lo me, God's handmaid!" In this sight I understood soothly
that she is more than all that God made beneath her in
worthiness and grace; for above her is nothing that is made
but the blessed [Manhood] of Christ, as to my sight.

## THE FIFTH CHAPTER

How God is to us everything that is good, tenderly
wrapping us

In this same time our Lord shewed me a ghostly sight of his
homely loving.

I saw that he is to us everything that is good and comfortable for us. He is our clothing that for love wrappeth
us, claspeth[1] us, and all becloseth us for tender love, that
he may never leave us; being to us all thing that is good, as
to mine understanding.

[1] MS. "halfyth us".

Also in this he shewed [me] a little thing, the quantity of an hazel-nut, in the palm of my hand; and it was as round as a ball. I looked thereupon with eye of my understanding, and thought: "What may this be?" And it was generally answered thus: "It is all that is made." I marvelled how it might last, for methought it might suddenly have fallen to naught for little[ness]. And I was answered in my understanding: "It lasteth, and ever shall [last] for that God loveth it." And so all thing hath the Being by the love of God.

In this Little Thing I saw three properties. The first is that God made it: the second is that God loveth it: the third, that God keepeth it. But what is to me soothly the Maker, the Keeper, and the Lover,—I cannot tell; for till I am substantially oned[1] to him, I may never have full rest nor very bliss: that is to say, till I be so fastened to him, that there is right naught that is made betwixt my God and me.

It needeth us to have knowing of the littleness of creatures and to naughten[2] all thing that is made, for to love and have God that is unmade. For this is the cause why we be not all in ease of heart and soul: that we seek here rest in those things that be so little, wherein is no rest, and know not our God that is Almighty, All-wise, All-good. For he is the Very Rest. God will[eth to] be known, and it liketh him that we rest in him; for all that is beneath him sufficeth not us. And this is the cause why that no soul is rested till it is naughted of[3] all things that are made. When it is wilfully naughted, for love to have him that is all, then is it able to receive ghostly rest.

Also our Lord God shewed that it is full great pleasance to him that a silly soul come to him nakedly and plainly and homely. For this is the kind yearnings of the soul, by the touching of the Holy Ghost (as by the understanding that I

[1] i.e., united.        [2] i.e., to make naught of.
[3] i.e., emptied of, detached from.

9

have in this Shewing). "God, of thy Goodness, give me thyself: for thou art enough to me, and I may nothing ask that is less, that may be full worship to thee; and if I ask anything that is less, ever me wanteth,—but only in thee I have all."

And these words are full lovesome to the soul, and full near touch they the will of God and his Goodness. For his Goodness comprehendeth all his creatures and all his blessed works, and overpasseth[1] without end. For he is the endlessness, and he hath made us only to himself, and restored us by his blessed Passion, and keepeth us in his blessed love; and all this is of his Goodness.

## THE SIXTH CHAPTER

### How we should pray, and of the great tender love that our Lord hath to man's soul

THIS Shewing was made to learn our soul wisely to cleave to the Goodness of God.

And in that time the custom of our praying was brought to mind: how we use for lack of understanding and knowing of Love, to make many means.[2]

Then saw I soothly that it is more worship to God, and more very delight, that we faithfully pray[3] to himself of his Goodness and cleave thereto by his Grace, with true understanding, and steadfast by love, than if we made all the means that heart can think. For if we make all these means, it is too little, and not full worship to God: but in his Goodness is all the whole, and there faileth right naught.

[1] i.e., surpasseth.
[2] MS. "To make many menys", i.e., to offer up many petitions.
[3] i.e., pray with confidence.

For thus, as I shall say, came to my mind in the same time: We pray to God for[1] his holy flesh and for his precious blood, his holy Passion, his dearworthy death and wounds: and all the blessed kindness,[2] the endless life that we have of all this, is [of] his Goodness. And we pray him for his sweet Mother's love that him bare; and all the help we have of her is of his Goodness. And we pray by his holy Cross that he died on, and all the virtue and the help that we have of the Cross, it is of his Goodness. And on the same wise, all the help that we have of special saints and all the blessed Company of Heaven, the dearworthy love and endless friendship that we have of them, it is of his Goodness. For God of his Goodness hath ordained means to help us, wholly fair and many: of which the chief and principal mean is the blessed nature[3] that he took of the Maid, with all the means that go afore and some after which belong to our redemption and to endless salvation. Wherefore it pleaseth him that we seek him and worship by means,[4] understanding and knowing that he is the Goodness of all.

For the Goodness of God is the highest prayer, and it cometh down to the lowest part of our need. It quickeneth our soul and bringeth it on life, and maketh it for to waxen in grace and virtue. It is nearest in nature; and readiest in grace: for it is the same grace that the soul seeketh, and ever shall [seek] till we know verily that he hath us all in himself beclosed.

For he hath no despite of that he hath made, nor hath he any disdain to serve us at the simplest office that to our body belongeth in nature,[3] for love of the soul that he hath made to his own likeness.

For as the body is clad in the cloth, and the flesh in the skin, and the bones in the flesh, and the heart in the whole,[5]

[1] i.e., for the sake of.     [2] i.e., natural bond.     [3] MS. "kind".
[4] i.e., by prayers.     [5] MS. "the bouke", i.e., the bulk.

so are we, soul and body, clad in the Goodness of God, and enclosed. Yea, and more homely—for all these may waste and wear away, but the Goodness of God is ever whole—and more near to us, without any likeness; for truly our Lover desireth that our soul cleave to him with all its might, and that we be evermore cleaving to his Goodness. For of all things that heart may think, this pleaseth most God, and soonest speedeth [the soul].

For our soul is so specially loved of him that is highest, that it overpasseth the knowing of all creatures: that is to say, there is no creature that is made that may wot how much and how sweetly and how tenderly our Maker loveth us. And therefore we may with grace and his help stand in ghostly beholding, with everlasting marvelling in this high, overpassing, one, inestimable[1] Love that Almighty God hath to us of his Goodness. And therefore we may ask of our Lover with reverence all that we will.

For our kindly Will is to have God, and the Good Will of God is to have us; and we may never cease[2] from willing nor from longing, till we have him in fulness of joy: and then may we no more will.

For he willeth that we be occupied in knowing and loving till the time that we shall be fulfilled in Heaven; and therefore was this lesson of Love shewed, with all that followeth, as ye shall see. For the strength and the Ground of all was shewed in the First Sight. For of all things the beholding and the loving of the Maker maketh the soul to seem least in his own sight, and most filleth it with reverent dread and true meekness; with plenty of charity to his even-Christians.[3]

---

[1] Or, as in Cressy, "unmeasurable".    [2] MS. "blyn".
[3] MS. "to his even cristen"—fellow-Christians.

## THE SEVENTH CHAPTER

How our Lady, beholding the greatness of her Maker,
thought herself less: and how the most joy to man
is that God, most high and mighty, is homeliest and
most courteous

AND to learn us this, as to mine understanding, our Lord
God shewed our Lady Saint Mary in the same time: that is
to say, the high Wisdom and Truth she had in beholding of
her Maker so great, so high, so mighty, and so good. This
greatness and this nobleness of the beholding of God fulfilled
her of reverent dread, and with this she saw herself so little
and so low, so simple and so poor, in regard of[1] her Lord
God, that this reverent dread fulfilled her of meekness. And
thus, by this ground [of meekness] she was fulfilled of grace
and of all manner of virtues, and overpasseth all creatures.

In all the time that he shewed this that I have said now in
ghostly sight, I saw the bodily sight lasting of the plenteous
bleeding of the Head. The great drops of blood fell down
from under the Garland like pellets, seeming as it had come
out of the veins; and in the coming out they were brown-
red, for the blood was full thick; and in the spreading-
abroad they were bright-red; and when they came to the
brows, then they vanished; notwithstanding, the bleeding
continued till many things were seen and understood. The
fairness and the liveliness is like nothing but the same; the
plenteousness is like to the drops of water that fall off the
eaves after a great shower of rain, that fall so thick that no
man may number them with bodily wit; and for the roundness, they were like to the scale of herring, in the spreading
on the forehead. These three came to my mind in the time:
pellets, for roundness, in the coming out of the blood; the

[1] i.e., in comparison with.

scale of herring, in the spreading in the forehead, for roundness; the drops off eaves, for the plenteousness innumerable.

This Shewing was quick and life-like, and hideous[1] and
dreadful, sweet and lovely. And of all the sight it was most
comfort to me that our God and Lord, that is so reverend
and dreadful, is so homely and courteous: and this most
fulfilled me with comfort and secureness of soul.

And to the understanding of this he shewed this open
example.

It is the most worship that a solemn King or a great Lord
may do a poor servant if he will be homely with him, and
specially if he sheweth it himself, of a full true meaning, and
with a glad cheer, both privily and publicly.[2] Then thinketh
this poor creature thus: "And what might this noble Lord
do [of] more worship and joy to me than to shew me, that
am so simple, this marvellous homeliness? Soothly it is more
joy and liking to me than [if] he gave me great gifts and were
himself strange in manner."

This bodily example was shewed so highly that man's
heart might be ravished and almost forgetting itself for joy
of the great homeliness. Thus it fareth with our Lord Jesus
and with us. For soothly it is the most joy that may be, as
to my sight, that he that is highest and mightiest, noblest
and worthiest, is lowest and meekest, homeliest and most
courteous: and truly and soothly this marvellous joy shall
be shewn us all when we see him.

And this willeth our Lord, that we seek for and trust to,
joy and delight in him, comforting us and solacing us, as we
may, with his grace and with his help, unto the time that
we see it verily. For the most fulness of joy that we shall
have, as to my sight, is the marvellous courtesy and homeliness of our Father that is our Maker, in our Lord Jesus
Christ that is our Brother and our Saviour.

[1] i.e., horrifying.          [2] MS. "partie".

But this marvellous homeliness may no man wot of in this time of life, save he have it of special shewing of our Lord, or of great plenty of grace inwardly given of the Holy Ghost. But faith and belief with charity deserveth the meed: and so it is had, by grace; for in faith, with hope and charity, our life is grounded. The Shewing, made to whom that God will, plainly teacheth the same, opened and declared, with many privy points belonging to our Faith which be worshipful to know. And when the Shewing which is given in a time is passed and hid, then the faith keepeth [it] by grace of the Holy Ghost unto our life's end. And thus by the Shewing it is not other than the faith, nor less nor more; as it may be seen in our Lord's teaching[1] in the same matter, by then that it come to the end.

## THE EIGHTH CHAPTER

A recapitulation of that that is said, and how it was shewed to her generally for all

AND as long as I saw this sight of the plenteous bleeding of the Head I might never cease from[2] these words: "Benedicite, Domine!"

In which Shewing I understood six things. The first is, the tokens of the blessed Passion and the plenteous shedding of his precious blood. The second is, the Maiden that is his dearworthy Mother. The third is, the blissful Godhead that ever was, is, and ever shall be: Almighty, All-Wisdom, All-Love. The fourth is, all thing that he hath made.—For well I wot that heaven and earth and all that is made is great and large, fair and good; but the cause why it shewed so little to my sight was for that I saw it in the presence of him that

---

[1] MS. "meneing".      [2] MS. "stinte of".

is the Maker of all things: for to a soul that seeth the Maker of all, all that is made seemeth full little.—The fifth is: he that made all thing for love, by the same love keepeth [it], and it is kept and shall be without end. The sixth is, that God is all that is good, as to my sight, and the goodness that every thing hath, it is he.[1]

And all these our Lord shewed me in the first Sight, with time and space to behold it. And the bodily sight stinted,[2] but the ghostly sight dwelled in mine understanding, and I abode with reverent dread, joying in that I saw. And I desired, as I durst, to see more, if it were his will, or else [to see for] longer time the same.

In all this I was greatly stirred in charity to mine even-Christians, that they might see and know the same that I saw: for I would it were comfort to them. For all this Sight was shewed general.[3] Then said I to them that were about me: "It is to-day Doomsday with me." And this I said for that I weened to have died. (For that day that a man dieth, he is doomed[4] as he shall be without end, as to mine understanding.) This I said for that I would they [had] loved God the better, for to make them to have in mind that this life is short, as they might see in example. For in all this time I weened to have died; and that was marvel to me, and troublous partly: for methought this Vision was shewed for them that should live. And that which I say of me, I say in the person of all mine even-Christians: for I am taught in the ghostly Shewing of our Lord God that he meaneth so. And therefore I pray you all for God's sake, and counsel you for your own profit, that ye leave the beholding of a wretch that it was shewed to, and mightily, wisely, and meekly behold God that of his courteous love and endless goodness

[1] MS. "God is althing that is gode, as to my sight, and the godenes that al thing hath, it is he".

[2] i.e., ceased.     [3] i.e., for all.     [4] MS. "deemed".

would shew it generally, in comfort of us all. For it is God's will that ye take it with great joy and liking, as if Jesus had shewed it unto you all.

## THE NINTH CHAPTER

Of the meekness of this woman, keeping her alway in the faith of Holy Church; and how he that loveth his even-Christian for God loveth all things

BECAUSE of the Shewing I am not good but if[1] I love God the better: and in as much as ye love God the better, it is more to you than to me. I say[2] not this to them that be wise, for they wot it well; but I say it to you that be simple, for ease and comfort: for we are all one in comfort. For soothly it was not shewed me that God loved me better than the least soul that is in grace; for I am sure that there be many that never had Shewing nor sight but of the common teaching of Holy Church, that love God better than I. For if I look singularly to myself, I am right naught; but in general I am in hope, in oneness of charity with all mine even-Christians.

For in this oneness standeth the life of all mankind that shall be saved. For God is all that is good, as to my sight, and God hath made all that is made, and God loveth all that he hath made: and he that loveth generally all his even-Christians for God, he loveth all that is. For in mankind that shall be saved is comprehended all: that is to say, all that is made and the Maker of all. For in man is God, and God is in all. And I hope by the grace of God he that beholdeth it thus shall be truly taught and mightily comforted, if he needeth comfort.

[1] i.e., unless.        [2] MS. "sey", i.e., *speak* or *tell*.

I speak of them that shall be saved, for in this time God shewed me none other. But in all things I believe as Holy Church believeth, preacheth, and teacheth. For the Faith of Holy Church, the which I had aforehand understood and, as I hope, by the grace of God willingly kept in use and custom, stood continually in my sight: [I] willing and meaning never to receive anything that might be contrary thereunto, and with this intent I beheld the Shewing with all my diligence: for in all this blessed Shewing I beheld it as one in God's meaning.[1]

All this was shewed by three [ways]: that is to say, by bodily sight, and by word formed in mine understanding, and by ghostly sight. But the ghostly sight I cannot nor may not shew it as openly nor as fully as I would. But I trust in our Lord God Almighty that he shall of his goodness, and for your love, make you to take it more ghostly and more sweetly than I can or may tell it.


## THE TENTH CHAPTER

The Second Revelation is of his discolouring, and of our
Redemption, and the discolouring of the Vernacle, and
how it pleaseth God that we seek him busily

AND after this I saw with bodily sight in the face of the crucifix that hung before me (on the which I beheld continually) a part of his Passion:—despite, spitting and sullying, and buffeting, and many lingering pains more than I can tell, and often changing of colour. And one time I saw how half the face, beginning at the ear, [was] overspread with dry blood till it covered to the mid-face. And after

[1] i.e., the teaching of the Catholic Faith and the teaching of the special Shewing were beheld as one.

that the other half [was] covered on the same wise, the whiles in this [first] part [it vanished] even as it came.

This saw I bodily, dimly,[1] and darkly; and I desired more bodily sight, to have seen more clearly. And I was answered in my reason: "If God will shew thee more, he shall be thy light: thee needeth none but him." For I saw him sought.[2]

For we are now so blind and unwise that we never seek God till he of his goodness sheweth him[self] to us. And when we aught see of him graciously, then are we stirred by the same grace to seek with great desire to see him more blissfully.

And thus I saw him and sought him; and I had him and I wanted him. And this is, and should be, our common working in this as to my sight.

One time mine understanding was led down into the sea-ground, and there I saw hills and dales green, seeming as it were moss-be-grown, with wrack and gravel. Then I understood thus: that if a man or woman were under the broad water, if he might have sight of God so as God is with a man continually, he should be safe in body and soul, and take no harm: and overpassing, he should have more solace and comfort than all this world can tell. For he willeth we believe that we see him continually, though that to us it seemeth but little; and in this belief he maketh us evermore to gain grace. For he will be seen and he will be sought: he will be abided and he will be trusted.

This Second Shewing was so low and so little and so simple, that my spirits were in great travail in the beholding,—mourning, dread-full, and longing—for I was some time in doubt whether it was a Shewing. And then diverse times our good Lord gave me more sight, whereby I understood truly that it was a Shewing. It was a figure and likeness

[1] MS. "swemely".

[2] Or, as in Cressy's version: "I saw him and sought him."

of our foul deeds' shame that our fair, bright, blessed Lord
bare for our sins. It made me to think of the Holy Vernacle[1]
of Rome: which he hath portrayed with his own blessed
face when he was in his hard Passion, wilfully going to his
death, and often changing of colour. Of the brownness and
blackness, the ruefulness and leanness of this Image many
marvel how it might be, since that he portrayed it with his
blessed Face who is the fairness of heaven, flower of earth,
and the fruit of the Maiden's womb. Then how might this
Image be so discolouring and so far from fair?—I desire to
say like as I have understood by the grace of God.

We know in our Faith, and believe by the teaching and
preaching of Holy Church, that the blessed Trinity made
Mankind to his image and to his likeness. In the same
manner-wise we know that, when man fell so deep and so
wretchedly by sin, there was none other help to restore man
but through him that made man. And he that made man for
love, by the same love he would restore man to the same
bliss, and overpassing. And like as we were like-made to
the Trinity in our first making, our Maker would that we
should be like Jesus Christ, our Saviour, in heaven without
end, by the virtue of our again-making.

Then atwixt these two, he would for love and worship of
man make himself as like to man in this deadly life, in our
foulness and our wretchedness, as man might be without
guilt. Wherefore it meaneth, as was said afore, that it was
the image and likeness of our foul black deeds' shame
wherein our fair, bright, blessed Lord God was hid. But
full sure I dare say, and we ought to trow it, that so fair a
man was never none but he, till what time his fair colour
was changed with travail and sorrow and Passion and dying.
Of this it is spoken in the Eighth Revelation, where it
treateth more of the same likeness. And where it sayeth of

[1] The Handkerchief of St Veronica, preserved at St Peter's.

the Vernacle of Rome, it meaneth by [reason of] diverse changing of colour and cheer, sometime more comfortably and lively, sometime more ruefully and deadly, as it may be seen in the Eighth Revelation.

And this vision was a learning, to mine understanding, that the continual seeking of the soul pleaseth God full greatly: for it may do no more than seek, suffer, and trust. And this is wrought in the soul that hath it, by the Holy Ghost; and the clearness of finding, it is of his special grace, when it is his will. The seeking, with faith, hope, and charity, pleaseth our Lord, and the finding pleaseth the soul and fulfilleth it with joy. And thus was I learned, to mine understanding, that seeking is as good as beholding, for the time that he will suffer the soul to be in travail. It is God's will that we seek him, to the beholding of him, forby that he shall shew us himself of his special grace when he will.[1] And how a soul shall have him in its beholding, he shall teach himself: and that is most worship to him and profit to thyself, and [the soul then] most receiveth of meekness and virtues with the grace and leading of the Holy Ghost. For a soul that only fasteneth it[self] on to God with very trust, either by seeking or in beholding, it is the most worship that it may do to him, as to my sight.

These are two workings that may be seen in this Vision: the one is seeking, the other is beholding. The seeking is common,—that every soul may have with his grace,—and ought to have that discretion and teaching of the Holy Church. It is God's will that we have three things in our seeking:—The first is that we seek wilfully and busily, without sloth, as it may be through his grace, gladly and merrily without unskilful heaviness and vain sorrow. The second is that we abide him steadfastly for his love, without grudging

[1] i.e., besides which he will shew us himself as a special favour when he will.

and striving against him, to our life's end: for it shall last but a while. The third is that we trust in him mightily of full sure faith, for it is his will. We know he shall appear suddenly and blissfully to all that be his lovers.

For his working is privy, and he willeth to be perceived; and his appearing shall be sweet and sudden; and he will be trusted. For he is full kind and homely: blessed may he be!

## THE ELEVENTH CHAPTER

*The Third Revelation is how God doth all things except sin, never changing his purpose without end: for he hath made all things in fulness of goodness*

AND after this I saw God in a Point,[1] that is to say, in mine understanding,—by which sight I saw that he is in all things.

I beheld with advisedness, seeing and knowing in [that] sight, with a soft dread; and thought: "What is sin?"

For I saw truly that God doeth all thing, be it never so little. And I saw truly that nothing is done by hap nor by adventure, but all things by the foreseeing wisdom of God: if it be hap or adventure in the sight of man, our blindness and our unforesight is the cause. For the things that are in the foreseeing wisdom of God from without beginning (which rightfully and worshipfully and continually he leadeth to the best end, as they come about), fall to us suddenly, ourselves unwitting. And thus by our blindness and our unforesight we say: these be haps and adventures: but to our Lord God they be not so.

Wherefore me behoveth needs to grant that all thing that is done, it is well done: for our Lord God doeth all. For in this time the working of creatures was not shewed, but [the

[1] i.e., all his divers perfections summed up in a single centre.

working] of our Lord God in the creature: for he is in the Mid-point of all thing, and all he doeth. And I was sure he doeth no sin.

And here I saw verily that sin is no deed: for in all this was not sin shewed. And I would no longer marvel in this, but beheld our Lord, what he would shew.

And thus, as it might be for the time, the rightfulness of God's working was shewed to the soul.

Rightfulness hath two fair properties: it is right and it is full; and so are all the works of our Lord God. Thereto needeth neither the working of mercy nor grace: for they be all rightful: wherein faileth naught.

But in another time he gave a Shewing for the beholding of sin nakedly, as I shall say: where he useth working of mercy and grace.

And this vision was shewed, to mine understanding: for our Lord will have the soul turned truly unto the beholding of him, and generally of all his works. For they are full good; and all his doings be easy and sweet, and to great ease bringing the soul that is turned from the beholding of the blind deeming of man unto the fair sweet deeming of our Lord God. For a man beholdeth some deeds well done and some deeds evil, but our Lord beholdeth them not so: for as all that hath being in kind is of God's making, so all that is done is in property of God's doing. For it is easy to understand that the best deed is well done: and so well as the best deed is done and the highest, so well is the least deed done; and all in property and in the order that our Lord hath ordained it to from without beginning. For there is no doer but he.

I saw full surely that he changeth never his purpose in no manner [of] thing, nor never shall, without end. For there was no thing unknown to him in his rightful ordinance from without beginning. And therefore all thing was set in order ere anything was made, as it should stand without end; and no manner [of] thing shall fail at that point. For he made all things in fulness of goodness, and therefore the blessed Trinity is ever full pleased in all his works.

And all this shewed he full blissfully, meaning thus: "See! I am God: see! I am in all thing: see! I do all thing: see! I lift never mine hands off my works, nor ever shall, without end: see! I lead all thing to the end I ordained it to from without beginning, by the same Might, Wisdom, and Love whereby I made it. How should any thing be amiss?"

Thus mightily, wisely, and lovingly was the soul examined in this Vision. Then saw I soothly that me behoved, of need, to assent, with great reverence and joying in God.


## THE TWELFTH CHAPTER

The Fourth Revelation is how it liketh God rather and better to wash us in his Blood from sin, than in water: for his Blood is most precious

AND after this I saw, beholding, the body plenteously bleeding in seeming of[1] the Scourging, as thus: the fair skin was broken full deep into the tender flesh with sharp smiting all about the sweet body. So plenteously the hot blood ran out that there was neither seen skin nor wound, but as it were all blood. And when it came where it should have fallen down, then it vanished. Notwithstanding, the bleeding continued awhile: till it might be seen with avisement. And this was so plenteous, to my sight, that methought if it had been so in kind[2] and in substance at that time, it should have made the bed all one blood, and have passed over about.

And then came to my mind that God hath made waters plenteous in earth to our service and to our bodily ease for

---

[1] i.e., as it were from.      [2] i.e., in reality.

tender love that he hath to us, but yet liketh him better that we take full homely his blessed blood to wash us of sin: for there is no water[1] that is made that he liketh so well to give us. For it is most plenteous as it is most precious: and that by the virtue of his blessed Godhead; and it is [of] our kind, and all-blissfully belongeth to us by the virtue of his precious love.

The dearworthy blood of our Lord Jesus Christ as verily as it is most precious, so verily it is most plenteous. Behold and see! The precious plenty of his dearworthy blood descended down into Hell and burst her bands and delivered all that were there which belonged to the Court of Heaven. The precious plenty of his dearworthy blood overfloweth all Earth, and is ready to wash all creatures of sin, which be of goodwill, have been, and shall be. The precious plenty of his dearworthy blood ascended up into Heaven to the blessed body of our Lord Jesus Christ, and there is in him, bleeding and praying for us to the Father—and is, and ever shall be as long as it needeth. And evermore it floweth in all Heavens enjoying the salvation of all mankind, that are there, and shall be—fulfilling the number[2] that faileth.

## THE THIRTEENTH CHAPTER

The Fifth Revelation is that the temptation of the fiend is overcome by the Passion of Christ, to the increase of our joy and of his pain, everlastingly

AND after this, ere God shewed any words, he suffered me to behold him for a convenient time, and all that I had seen, and all intellect[3] that was therein, as the simplicity of the

---

[1] MS. "licor".       [2] The appointed number of the saints.
[3] i.e., the meaning.

soul might take it.[1] Then he, without voice and opening of lips, formed in my soul these words: "Herewith is the Fiend overcome." These words said our Lord, meaning his blessed Passion as he shewed it afore.

On this shewed our Lord that the Passion of him is the overcoming of the Fiend. God shewed that the Fiend hath now the same malice that he had afore the Incarnation. And as sore he travaileth, and as continually he seeth that all souls of salvation escape him, worshipfully, by the virtue of Christ's precious Passion. And that is his sorrow, and full evil is he ashamed: for all that God suffereth him to do turneth [for] us to joy and [for] him to shame and woe. And he hath as much sorrow when God giveth him leave to work, as when he worketh not: and that is for that he may never do as evil as he would: for his might is all taken into God's hand.

But in God there may be no wrath, as to my sight: for our good Lord endlessly hath regard to his own worship and to the profit of all that shall be saved. With might and right he withstandeth the Reproved, the which of malice and shrewdness busy them to contrive and to do against God's will. Also I saw our Lord scorn his malice and naught his unmight; and he willeth that we do so. For this sight I laughed mightily, and that made them to laugh that were about me, and their laughing was a liking to me. I thought that I would that all mine even-Christians had seen as I saw, and then would they all laugh with me. But I saw not Christ laugh. For I understood that we may laugh in comforting of ourselves and joying in God for [that] the devil is overcome. And when I saw him scorn his malice, it was by leading of mine understanding unto our Lord: that is to say, [it was] an inward shewing of verity, without changing of cheer.[2]

[1] i.e., in so far as my simple soul was able to understand it.

[2] MS. "chere", i.e., expression of countenance.

For, as to my sight, it is a worshipful property of God that [he] is ever the same.[1]

And after this I fell into a sadness, and said: "I see three things: game, scorn, and earnest. I see [a] game, [in] that the Fiend is overcome; I see scorn, [in] that God scorneth him, and he shall be scorned; and I see earnest, [in] that he is overcome by the blissful Passion and Death of our Lord Jesus Christ that was done in full earnest and with sad travail."

When I said, "he is scorned,"—I meant that God scorneth him, that is to say, because he seeth him now as he shall do without end. For in this [word] God shewed that the Fiend is damned. And this meant I when I said: "he shall be scorned:" [because he shall be scorned] at Doomsday, generally of all that shall be saved, to whose consolation he hath great envy. For then he shall see that all the woe and tribulation that he hath done to them shall be turned to increase of their joy, without end; and all the pain and tribulation that he would have brought them to shall endlessly go with him to hell.


## THE FOURTEENTH CHAPTER

The Sixth Revelation is of the worshipful thanks with which he rewardeth his servants, and how it hath three joys

AFTER this our good Lord said: "I thank thee for thy travail, namely [that] of thy youth."

And in this [Shewing] mine understanding was lifted up into Heaven where I saw our Lord as a lord in his own house, who hath called all his dearworthy servants and friends to a

[1] MS. "it is a worshipful property that is in God which is durable".

solemn feast. Then I saw the Lord take no place in his own house, but I saw him royally reign in his house, fulfilling it with joy and mirth, himself endlessly to gladden and to solace his dearworthy friends, full homely and full courteously, with marvellous melody of endless love, in his own fair blessed Countenance.[1] Which glorious Countenance[1] of the Godhead fulfilleth Heaven with joy and bliss.

God shewed three degrees of bliss that every soul shall have in Heaven that wilfully hath served God in any degree in earth. The first is the worshipful thanks of our Lord God that he shall receive when he is delivered of pain. This thanking is so high and so worshipful that him thinketh it filleth him though there were no more. For methought that all the pain and travail that might be suffered of all living men might not deserve the worshipful thanks that one man shall have that wilfully hath served God. The second is that all the blessed creatures that are in Heaven shall see that worshipful thanking, and he maketh his service known to all that are in Heaven. And in this time this example was shewed: A king, if he thank his servants, it is a great worship to them, and if he maketh it known to all the realm, then is his worship greatly increased. The third is, that as new and as liking as it is received in that time, right so shall it last without end.

And I saw that homely and sweetly was this shewed, that the age of every man shall be [made] known in Heaven, and [he] shall be rewarded for his wilful service and for his time. And namely the age of them that willingly and freely offer their youth to God, passingly is rewarded and wonderly is thanked.

For I saw that whene'er what time a man or woman be truly turned to God,—for one day's service and for his endless will he shall have all these three degrees of bliss. And

[1] MS. "chere".

the more the loving soul seeth this courtesy of God, the liefer he[1] is to serve him all the days of his life.

## THE FIFTEENTH CHAPTER

The Seventh Revelation is of oftentimes feeling of weal and woe: and how it is expedient that man sometimes be left without comfort, and that sin is not the cause of this

AND after this he shewed a sovereign ghostly liking in my soul. I was fulfilled with the everlasting sureness, mightily sustained, without any painful dread. This feeling was so glad and so ghostly that I was in all peace and in rest, [so] that there was nothing in earth that should have grieved me.

This lasted but a while, and I was turned and left to myself in heaviness, and weariness of my life, and irksomeness of myself, [so] that scarcely I could have patience to live. There was no comfort nor none ease to me but faith, hope, and charity; and these I had in truth, but little in feeling.

And anon after this our blessed Lord gave me again the comfort and the rest in soul, in liking and sureness so blissful and so mighty that no dread, no sorrow, nor pain bodily that might be suffered should have dis-eased me. And then the pain shewed again to my feeling, and then the joy and the liking, and now that one, and now that other, divers times —I suppose about twenty times. And in the same time of joy I might have said with Saint Paul: "Nothing shall depart me from the charity of Christ"; and in the pain I might have said with Peter: "Lord, save me; I perish!"

This Vision was shewed me, after mine understanding,

---

[1] In the MS. *the soul* is usually referred to as "he"; "it" is also used in some passages.

[for] that it is speedful to some souls to feel on this wise: sometime to be in comfort, and sometime to fail and to be left to themselves. God willeth [that] we know that he keepeth us even alike secure in woe and in weal. And for profit of man's soul, a man is sometime left to himself; although sin is not always[1] the cause: for in this time I sinned not wherefore I should be left to myself—for it was so sudden. Also I deserved not to have this blessed feeling. But freely our Lord giveth when he will; and suffereth us [to be] in woe sometime. And both is one love.

For it is God's will [that] we hold us in comfort with all our might: for bliss is lasting without end, and pain is passing and shall be brought to naught for them that shall be saved. And therefore it is not God's will that we follow the feelings of pain in sorrow and mourning for them, but that suddenly passing over, [we] hold us in endless liking.

## THE SIXTEENTH CHAPTER

The Eighth Revelation is of the last piteous pains of Christ's dying and discolouring of his face and drying of his flesh

AFTER this Christ shewed a part of his Passion near his dying.

I saw his sweet face as it were dry and bloodless with pale dying. And later,[2] more pale, dead, languoring; and then turned more dead unto blue; and then more brown-blue, as the flesh turned more deeply dead. For his Passion shewed to me most specially[3] in his blessed face, and chiefly in his lips: there I saw these four colours, though it were afore fresh, ruddy, and liking, to my sight. This was a sorrowful

[1] MS. "ever".     [2] MS. "sithen".     [3] MS. "properly".

change to see, this deep dying. And also the nose clogged[1] and dried, to my sight, and the sweet body was brown and black, all turned out of fair, lively colour of itself, unto dry dying.

For that same time that our Lord and blessed Saviour died upon the Rood, it was a dry, hard wind, and wondrous cold, as to my sight, and what time the precious blood was bled out of the sweet body that might pass therefrom, yet there dwelled a moisture in the sweet flesh of Christ, as it was shewed.

Bloodlessness and pain dried within; and blowing of wind and cold coming from without met together in the sweet body of Christ. And these four,—twain without, and twain within—dried the flesh of Christ by process of time. And though this pain was bitter and sharp, it was full long lasting, as to my sight, and painfully dried up all the lively spirits of Christ's flesh. Thus I saw the sweet flesh dry in seeming by part after part: drying with marvellous pains. And as long as any spirit had life in Christ's flesh, so long suffered he pain.

This long pining seemed to me as if he had been seven nights dead, dying, at the point of outpassing away, suffering the last pain. And when I said it seemed to me as if he had been seven nights dead, it meaneth that the sweet body was so discoloured, so dry, so clogged, so deathly, and so piteous, as [if] he had been seven nights dead, continually dying. And methought the drying of Christ's flesh was the most pain, and the last, of his Passion.

[1] MS. "clange".

## THE SEVENTEENTH CHAPTER

*Of the grievous bodily thirst of Christ, caused four-wise, and of his piteous crowning, and of the most pain to a kind lover*

AND in this dying was brought to my mind the words of Christ: *"I thirst."*

For I saw in Christ a double thirst: one bodily; another ghostly, the which I shall speak of in the Thirty-first Chapter.

For this word was shewed for the bodily thirst: the which I understood was caused by failing of moisture. For the blessed flesh and bones was left all alone without blood and moisture. The blessed body dried alone long time, with wringing of the nails and weight of the body. For I understood that, for tenderness of the sweet hands and of the sweet feet, by the greatness, hardness, and grievousness of the nails the wounds waxed wide and the body sagged, for weight by long time hanging. And [therewith was] piercing and wringing of the head, and binding of the Crown all baked with dry blood, with the sweet hair clinging, and the dry flesh, to the thorns, and the thorns to the flesh drying; and in the beginning while the flesh was fresh and bleeding, the continual sitting of the thorns made the wounds wide. And furthermore I saw that the sweet skin and the tender flesh, with the hair and the blood, was all raised and loosed about from the bone, with the thorns wherethrough it were digged in many pieces, as a cloth that were sagging, as if it would hastily have fallen off, for heaviness and looseness, while it had natural[1] moisture. And that was great sorrow and dread to me: for methought I would not for my life have seen it fall. How it was done I saw not; but understood

[1] MS. "kind".

it was with the sharp thorns and the boisterous and grievous
setting on of the Garland [of Thorns] unsparingly and without pity. This continued awhile, and soon it began to change,
and I beheld and marvelled how it might be. And then I saw
it was because it began to dry, and stint a part of the weight,
and set about the Garland. And thus it environed all about,
as it were garland upon garland. The Garland of the Thorns
was dyed with the blood, and the other garland [of Blood]
and the head, all was one colour, as clotted blood when it is
dry. The skin of the flesh that shewed of the face and of the
body, was small-wrinkled with a tanned colour, like a dry
board when it is skinned;[1] and the face more brown than
the body.

I saw four manner of dryings: the first was bloodless; the
second was pain following after; the third, hanging up in
the air, as men hang a cloth to dry; the fourth, that the
bodily kind asked liquor and there was no manner of comfort ministered to him in all his woe and dis-ease. Ah! hard
and grievous was his pain, but much more hard and grievous
it was when the moisture failed and all began to dry thus
clinging.

These were the pains that shewed in the blessed head:
the first wrought to the dying, while it was moist; and that
other, slow, with clinging drying, with blowing of the wind
from without, that dried and pained him with cold more
than mine heart can think.

And other pains—for which pains I saw that all is too
little that I can say: for it may not be told.

The which Shewing of Christ's pains filled me full of pain.
For I wist well he suffered but once, but [this was as if] he
would shew it me and fill me with mind as I had afore desired.
And in all this time of Christ's pains I felt no pain but for
Christ's pains. Then thought-me: "I knew but little what

[1] i.e., when the bark is stripped off.

pain it was that I asked"; and, as a wretch, repented me, thinking: "If I had wist what it had been, loth me had been to have prayed it." For methought it passed bodily death, my pains.[1]

I thought: "Is any pain like this?" And I was answered in my reason: "Hell is another pain: for there is despair. But of all pains that lead to salvation this is the most pain, to see thy Love suffer. How might any pain be more to me than to see him that is all my life, all my bliss, and all my joy, suffer?" Here felt I soothfastly[2] that I loved Christ so much above myself that there was no pain that might be suffered like to that sorrow that I had to see him in pain.


## THE EIGHTEENTH CHAPTER

Of the spiritual martyrdom of our Lady and other lovers of Christ, and how all things suffered with him good and evil

HERE I saw a part of the compassion of our Lady, Saint Mary: for Christ and she were so oned in love that the greatness of her loving was cause of the greatness of her pain. For in this [Shewing] I saw a Substance of kind[3] Love, continued by Grace, that creatures have to him: which Kind Love was most fully shewed in his sweet Mother, and overpassing; for so much as she loved him more than all other, her pains passed all other's. For ever the higher, the mightier, the sweeter that the love be, the more sorrow it is to the lover to see that body in pain that is loved.

And all his disciples and all his true lovers suffered pains more than their own bodily dying. For I am sure by mine

---

[1] See Note 2, *infra*, p. 171.     [2] i.e., in truth.     [3] i.e., natural.

own feeling that the least of them loved him so far above himself that it passeth all that I can say.

Here saw I a great oneing betwixt Christ, and us, to mine understanding: for when he was in pain, we were in pain.

And all creatures that might suffer pain, suffered with him: that is to say, all creatures that God hath made to our service. The firmament, the earth, failed for sorrow in their kind in the time of Christ's dying. For it belongeth kindly to their property to know him for their God, in whom all their virtue standeth: when he failed, then behoved it needs to them for kindness to fail with him, as much as they might, for sorrow of his pains.

And thus they that were his friends suffered pain for love. And, generally, all: that is to say, they that knew him not suffered for failing of all manner of comfort save the mighty, privy keeping of God. I speak[1] of two manner of folk, as they may be understood by two persons: the one was Pilate, the other was Saint Dionyse[2] of France, which was [at] that time a Paynim. For when he saw wondrous and marvellous sorrows and dreads that befell in that time, he said: "Either the world is now at an end, or he that is Maker of Kind suffereth." Wherefore he did write on an altar: THIS IS THE ALTAR OF UNKNOWN GOD. God of his goodness maketh the planets and the elements to work of kind to the blessed man and the cursed, [but] in that time it was withdrawn from both; wherefore it was that they that knew him not were in sorrow that time.

Thus was our Lord Jesus naughted for us; and all we stand in this manner naughted with him, and shall do till we come to his bliss; as I shall tell after.

[1] MS. "mene".

[2] Julian, like other medieval writers, believed that St Denis of France was identical with Dionysius the Areopagite, mentioned in Acts xvii. 34.

## THE NINETEENTH CHAPTER

Of the comfortable beholding of the crucifix, and how
the desire of the flesh, without consent of the soul, is
no sin, and the flesh must be in pain, suffering till both
be oned to Christ

In this [time] I would have looked up from the Cross, but I
durst not. For I wist well that while I beheld in the Cross I
was sure and safe; therefore I would not assent to put my
soul in peril: for beside the Cross was no sureness, for fear[1]
of fiends.

Then had I a proffer in my reason as [if] it had been friendly
said to me: "Look up to Heaven to his Father." And then
saw I well, with the faith that I felt, that there was nothing
betwixt the Cross and Heaven that might have dis-eased me.
Either me behoved to look up or else to answer. I answered
inwardly with all the might of my soul, and said: "Nay; I
may not: for thou art my Heaven." This I said for [that] I
would not. For I would liever have been in that pain till
Doomsday than to come to Heaven otherwise than by him.
For I wist well that he that bound me so sore, he should un-
bind me when that he would. Thus was I learned to choose
Jesus to my Heaven, whom I saw only in pain at that time:
meliked no other Heaven than Jesus, which shall be my
bliss when I come there.

And this hath ever been a comfort to me, that I chose
Jesus to my Heaven, by his grace, in all this time of Passion
and sorrow; and that hath been a learning to me that I
should evermore do so: choosing only Jesus to my Heaven
in weal and woe.

And though I as a wretched creature had repented me—I
said afore if I had wist what pain it would be, I had been loth

[1] MS. "uggyng".

36

to have prayed—here saw I soothly that it was grudging and damning of the flesh without assent of the soul: to which God assigneth no blame. Repenting and wilful choice be two contraries which I felt both in one at that time. And these be [our] two parts: the one outward, the other inward. The outward part is our deadly flesh-hood, which is now in pain and woe, and shall be, in this life—whereof I felt much in this time—and that part it was that repented. The inward part is an high, blissful life, which is all in peace and in love: and this was more privily felt; and this part is [that] in which mightily, wisely, and wilfully I chose Jesus to my Heaven.

And in this I saw soothly that the inward part is master and sovereign to the outward, not charging itself with, nor taking heed to the will of that: but all the intent and will is set endlessly to be oned into our Lord Jesus. That the outward part should draw the inward to assent was not shewed to me; but that the inward draweth the outward by grace, and both shall be oned in bliss without end, by the virtue of Christ,—this was shewed.

## THE TWENTIETH CHAPTER

Of the unspeakable Passion of Christ, and of three things of the Passion always to be remembered

AND thus I saw our Lord Jesus languoring long time. For the oneing with the Godhead gave strength to the manhood for love to suffer more than all men might suffer. 1 mean not only more pain than all men might suffer, but also that he suffered more pain than all men of salvation that ever were from the first beginning unto the last day might tell or fully think, having regard to the worthiness of the highest worshipful King and the shameful, despiteous, painful death. For he that is highest and worthiest was most fulliest naughted and utterliest despised.

For the highest point that may be seen in the Passion is to think and know what he is that suffered. And in this [Shewing] he brought in part to mind the height and nobleness of the glorious Godhead, and therewith the preciousness and the tenderness of the blissful Body, which be together oned; and also the lothness that is in our kind to suffer pain. For as much as he was most tender and clean, right so he was most strong and mighty to suffer.

And for every man's sin that shall be saved he suffered: and every man's sorrow and desolation he saw, and sorrowed for kindness and love. (For in as much as our Lady sorrowed for his pains, in so much he suffered sorrow for her sorrow; and more, in as much as the sweet manhood of him was worthier in kind.) For as long as he was passible he suffered for us and sorrowed for us; and now he is uprisen and no more passible, yet he suffereth with us.

And I, beholding all this by his grace, saw that the Love of him was so strong, which he hath to our soul, that wilfully he chose it with great desire, and mildly he suffered it with well-paining.

For the soul that beholdeth it thus, when it is touched by grace, it shall verily see that the pains of Christ's Passion pass all pains: [all our pains] that is to say, which shall be turned into everlasting, surpassing joys by the virtue of Christ's Passion.

## THE TWENTY-FIRST CHAPTER

Of three beholdings in the Passion of Christ, and how
we were dying on the cross with Christ; but his cheer
putteth away all pain

'Tis God's will, as to mine understanding, that we have
Three Manners of Beholding his blessed Passion. The First
is: [beholding] the hard Pain that he suffered, with contrition and compassion. And that shewed our Lord in this time,
and gave me might and grace to see it.

And I looked for the departing with all my might, and
thought to have seen the body all dead; but I saw him not so.
And right in the same time that methought, by the seeming,
the life might no longer last and the Shewing of the end
behoved needs to be,—suddenly (I beholding in the same
Cross), he changed [to] his blissful cheer. The changing of
his blessed Countenance changed mine, and I was as glad and
merry as it was possible. Then brought our Lord merrily to
my mind: "Where is now any point of thy pain, or of thy
grief?" And I was full merry.

I understood that we be now, in our Lord's meaning, in
his Cross with him in our pains and our Passion, dying; and
we, wilfully abiding in the same Cross with his help and his
grace unto the last point, suddenly he shall change his Cheer
to us, and we shall be with him in Heaven. Betwixt that one
and that other shall be no time, and then shall all be brought
to joy. And so meant he in this Shewing: "Where is now any
point of thy pain, or thy grief?" And we shall be full blessed.

And here saw I soothfastly that if he shewed now [to] us
his blissful Cheer, there is no pain in earth or in other place
that should aggrieve us; but all things should be to us joy
and bliss. But because he sheweth to us time of his Passion,
as he bare [it] in this life, and his Cross, therefore we are in

39

dis-ease and travail with him, as our frailty asketh. And the
cause why he suffereth [it to be so,] is for [that] he will of
his goodness make us the higher with him in his bliss; and
for this little pain that we suffer here, we shall have an high
endless knowing in God which we might never have without
that. And the harder our pains have been with him in his
Cross, the more shall our worship[1] be with him in his Kingdom.

## THE TWENTY-SECOND CHAPTER

The Ninth Revelation is the looking of three heavens,
and the infinite love of Christ desiring every day to
suffer for us if he might, although it is not needful

THEN said our good Lord Jesus Christ: "Art thou well paid
that I suffered for thee?" I said: "Yea, good Lord, gramercy.
Yea, good Lord, blessed mayst thou be." Then said Jesus,
our kind Lord: "If thou art paid, I am paid: it is a joy, a bliss,
and endless liking to me that ever suffered I passion for thee;
and if I might suffer more, I would suffer more."

In this feeling my understanding was lifted up into
Heaven, and there I saw three heavens: of which sight I
greatly marvelled. And though I see three heavens—and all
in the blessed manhood of Christ—none is more, none is
less, none is higher, none is lower, but [all] even-like in
bliss.

For the First Heaven, Christ shewed me his Father; in no
bodily likeness, but in his property and in his working. That
is to say, I saw in Christ that the Father is. The working of
the Father is this, that he giveth meed to his Son, Jesus
Christ. This gift and this meed is so blissful to Jesus that his
Father might have given him no meed that might have liked

[1] i.e., glory.

him better. The first heaven, that is the pleasing of the Father, shewed to me as one heaven; and it was full blissful: for he is full pleased with all the deeds that Jesus hath done about our salvation. Wherefore we be not only his by his buying, but also by the courteous gift of his Father we be his bliss, we be his meed, we be his worship, we be his crown— and this was a singular marvel and a full delectable beholding that we be his crown! This that I say is so great bliss to Jesus that he setteth at naught all his travail, and his hard Passion, and his cruel and shameful death.

And in these words: "If that I might suffer more, I would suffer more,"—I saw soothly that as often as he might die, so often he would, and love should never let him have rest till he had done it. And I beheld with great diligence for to learn how often he would die if he might. And soothly the number passed mine understanding and my wits so far that my reason might not, nor could comprehend it. And when he had thus oft died, or should, yet he would set it at naught for love: for all seemeth him but little in comparison with his love.[1]

For though the sweet manhood of Christ might suffer but once, the goodness in him may never cease of proffer: every day he is ready to the same, if it might be. For if he said he would for my love make new Heavens and new Earth, it were but little in comparison;[2] for this might be done every day if he would, without any travail. But to die for my love so often that the number passeth creature's reason, it is the highest proffer that our Lord God might make to man's soul, as to my sight. Then meaneth he thus: "How should it then be that I should not do for thy love all that I might which deed grieveth me not, sith I would, for thy love, die so often, having no regard[3] to my hard pains?"

[1] MS. "ffor al thynketh him but litil in reward of his love".
[2] MS. "reward".     [3] MS. "reward".

And here saw I, for the Second Beholding in this blessed Passion, the love that made him to suffer passeth as far all his pains as Heaven is above Earth. For the pains was a noble, worshipful deed done in a time by the working of love: and Love was without beginning, is, and shall be without ending. For which love he said full sweetly these words: "If I might suffer more, I would suffer more." He said not, "If it were needful to suffer more": for though it were not needful, if he might suffer more, he would.

This deed, and this work about our salvation, was ordained as well as God might ordain it. And here I saw a full bliss in Christ: for his bliss should not have been full, if it might any better have been done.


## THE TWENTY-THIRD CHAPTER

How Christ willeth that we joy with him greatly in our Redemption and desire grace of him that we may do so

AND in these three words: "It is a joy, a bliss, an endless liking to me," were shewed three heavens, as thus: for the joy, I understood the pleasure of the Father; and for the bliss, the worship of the Son; and for the endless liking, the Holy Ghost. The Father is pleased, the Son is worshipped, the Holy Ghost liketh.

And here saw I, for the Third Beholding in his blissful Passion: that is to say, the Joy and the Bliss that make him to liken it. For our Courteous Lord shewed his Passion to me in five manners: of which the first is the bleeding of the head; the second is discolouring of his face; the third is the plenteous bleeding of the body, in seeming of the scourging; the fourth is the deep dying:—these four are aforesaid for the pains of the Passion. And the fifth is [this] that was shewed for the joy and the bliss of the Passion.

For it is God's will that we have true liking with him in our salvation, and therein he willeth [that] we be mightily comforted and strengthened; and thus willeth he merrily with his grace that our soul be occupied. For we are his bliss: for in us he liketh without end; and so shall we in him, with his grace.

And all that he hath done for us, and doeth, and ever shall, was never cost nor charge to him, nor might be, but only that [which] he did in our manhood, beginning at the sweet Incarnation and lasting to the Blessed Uprise on Easter-morrow:[1] so long dured the cost and the charge about our redemption in deed: of [the] which deed he enjoyeth endlessly, as it is aforesaid.

Jesus willeth [that] we take heed to the bliss that is in the blissful Trinity [because] of our salvation, and that we desire to have as much ghostly liking, with his grace, as it is aforesaid: that is to say, that the liking of our salvation be [as] like to the joy that Christ hath of our salvation as it may be while we are here.

All the Trinity wrought in the Passion of Christ, ministering abundance of virtues and plenty of grace to us by him: but only the Maiden's Son suffered: whereof all the blessed Trinity endlessly enjoyeth. All this was shewed in these words: "Art thou well paid?"—and by that other word that Christ said: "If thou art paid, then am I paid;"—as if he said: "It is joy and liking enough to me, and I ask naught else of thee for my travail but that I might well pay thee."

And in this he brought to mind the property of a glad giver. A glad giver taketh but little heed of the thing that he giveth, but all his desire and all his intent is to please him and solace him to whom he giveth it. And if the receiver

[1] MS. "Esterne morrow".

43

take the gift highly and thankfully, then the courteous giver
setteth at naught all his cost and all his travail, for joy and
delight that he hath pleased and solaced him that he loveth.
Plenteously and fully was this shewed.

Think also wisely of the greatness of this word "ever".
For in it was shewed an high knowing of love that he hath in
our salvation, with manifold joys that follow of the Passion
of Christ. One is that he joyeth that he hath done it in deed,
and he shall no more suffer; another, that he hath brought
us up into heaven and made us for to be his crown and endless
bliss; another, that he hath therewith bought us from endless pains of hell.


## THE TWENTY-FOURTH CHAPTER

The Tenth Revelation is that our Lord Jesus Christ
sheweth in love his blessed Heart cloven in two,
rejoicing

THEN with a glad cheer our Lord looked unto his Side and
beheld, rejoicing. With his sweet looking he led forth the
understanding of his creature by the same wound into his
Side within. And then he shewed a fair, delectable place,
and large enough for all mankind that shall be saved to rest
in peace and in love. And therewith he brought to mind his
dearworthy blood and precious water which he let pour
all out for love. And with the sweet beholding he shewed
his blissful heart even cloven in two.

And with this sweet enjoying, he shewed unto mine
understanding, in part, the blessed Godhead, stirring then
the poor soul for to understand, as it may be said, that is, to
think on the endless Love[1] that was without beginning, and

[1] MS. "that is to mene the endles love".

44

is, and shall be ever. And with this our good Lord said full blissfully: "Lo, how that I loved thee," as if he had said: "My darling, behold and see thy Lord, thy God that is thy Maker and thine endless joy, see what liking and bliss I have in thy salvation; and for my love enjoy now with me."

And also, for more understanding, this blessed word was said: "Lo, how I loved thee! Behold and see that I loved thee so much ere I died for thee, that I would die for thee; and now I have died for thee and suffered willingly that [which] I may. And now is all my bitter pain and all my hard travail turned to endless joy and bliss to me and to thee. How should it now be that thou shouldst anything pray that liketh me, but that I should full gladly grant it thee? For my liking is thy holiness and thine endless joy and bliss with me."

This is the understanding, simply as I can say, of this blessed word: "Lo, how I loved thee." This shewed our good Lord for to make us glad and merry.


## THE TWENTY-FIFTH CHAPTER

### The Eleventh Revelation is an high ghostly shewing of his blessed Mother

AND with this same cheer of mirth and joy our good Lord looked down on the right side and brought to my mind where our Lady stood in the time of his Passion; and said: "Wilt thou see her?" And in this sweet word [it was] as if he had said: "I wot well thou wouldst see my blessed Mother: for, after myself, she is the highest joy that I might shew thee, and most liking and worship to me; and most she is desired to be seen of my blessed creatures." And for the high, marvellous, singular love that he hath to this sweet Maiden, his blessed Mother, our Lady Saint Mary, he shewed her highly rejoicing as by the meaning of these sweet words; as if he said: "Wilt thou see how I love her, that thou mightest joy with me in the love that I have in her and she in me?"

And also (to more understanding this sweet word) our Lord God speaketh to all mankind that shall be saved, as it were all to one person, as if he said: "Wilt thou see in her how thou art loved? For thy love I made her so high, so noble and so worthy; and this liketh me, and so will I that it doth thee." For after himself she is the most blissful sight.

But hereof am I not learned so long to see her bodily presence while I am here, but the virtues of her blessed soul: her truth, her wisdom, her charity; whereby I may learn to know myself and reverently dread my God. And when our good Lord had shewed this and said this word: "Wilt thou see her?" I answered and said: "Yea, good Lord, gramercy: yea, good Lord, if it be thy will." Oftentimes I prayed this, and I weened to have seen her in bodily presence, but I saw her not so. And Jesus in that word shewed me ghostly sight of her: right as I had seen her afore, little and simple, so he shewed her then, high and noble and glorious, and pleasing to him above all creatures.

And he willeth that it be known; that [so] all those that like in him should liken them in her, and in the liking that he hath in her and she in him. And, to more understanding, he shewed this example: As if a man love a creature singularly, above all creatures, he will make all creatures to love and to like that creature that he loveth so greatly. And in this word that Jesus said: "Wilt thou see her?" methought it was the most liking word that he might have given me of her, with the ghostly Shewing that he gave me of her. For our Lord shewed me nothing in special but our Lady Saint Mary; and her he shewed three times. The first was as she was with Child; the second was as she was in her sorrows under the Cross; the third is as she is now in pleasing, worship, and joy.

## THE TWENTY-SIXTH CHAPTER

### The Twelfth Revelation is that the Lord our God is all Sovereign Being

AND after this our Lord shewed him[self] more glorified, as to my sight, than I saw him before [in the Shewing] wherein I was learned that our soul shall never have rest till it cometh to him, knowing that he is fulness of joy, homely and courteous, blissful and very life.

Our Lord Jesus oftentimes said: "I it am, I it am: I it am that is highest, I it am that thou lovest, I it am that thou likest, I it am that thou servest, I it am that thou longest for, I it am that thou desirest, I it am that thou meanest, I it am that is all. I it am that Holy Church preacheth and teacheth thee, I it am that shewed me here to thee." The number of the words passeth my wit and all my understanding and all my might. And they are the highest, as to my sight: for therein is comprehended—I cannot tell,—but the joy that I saw in the Shewing of them passeth all that heart may wish for and soul may desire. Therefore the words be not declared here; but [let] every man, after the grace that God giveth him in understanding and loving, receive them in our Lord's meaning.

## THE TWENTY-SEVENTH CHAPTER

*The Thirteenth Revelation is that our Lord God willeth that we have great regard to all his deeds that he hath done in the great nobility of making all things, and how sin is not known but by the pain*

AFTER this the Lord brought to my mind the longing that I had to him afore. And I saw that nothing letted me but sin. And so I beheld, generally, in us all, and methought: "If sin had not been, we should all have been clean and like to our Lord, as he made us."

And thus, in my folly, afore this time often I wondered why by the great foreseeing wisdom of God the beginning of sin was not letted: for then, methought, all should have been well. This stirring [of wonder] was much to be forsaken, but nevertheless mourning and sorrow I made therefor, without reason and discretion.

But Jesus, who in this Vision informed me of all that me needeth, answered by this word and said: "It behoved that there should be sin; but all shall be well, and all shall be well, and all manner of thing shall be well."[1]

In this naked word *sin*, our Lord brought to my mind, generally, all that is not good, and the shameful despite and the utter naughting that he bare for us in this life, and his dying; and all the pains and passions of all his creatures, ghostly and bodily; (for we be all partly naughted, and we shall be naughted following our Master, Jesus, till we be full purged, that is to say, till we be fully naughted of our deadly flesh and of all our inward affections which be not very good;) and the beholding of this, with all pains that ever were or ever shall be,—and with all these I understand the

[1] MS. "Synne is behovabil, but al shal be wel & al shal be wel & al manner of thyng shal be wele."

Passion of Christ for most pain, and overpassing. All this was shewed in a touch and readily passed over into comfort; for our good Lord would not that the soul were affeared of this ugly sight. .

But I saw not sin: for I believe it hath no manner of substance nor no part of being, nor could it be known but by the pain that it is cause of.

And thus pain, it is something, as to my sight, for a time; for it purgeth, and maketh us to know ourselves and to ask mercy. For the Passion of our Lord is comfort to us against all this, and so is his blessed will. And for the tender love that our good Lord hath to all that shall be saved, he comforteth readily and sweetly, meaning thus: "It is sooth[1] that sin is cause of all this pain; but all shall be well, and all shall be well, and all manner [of] thing shall be well."

These words were said full tenderly, showing no manner of blame to me nor to any that shall be saved. Then were it a great unkindness[2] to blame or wonder on God for my sin, since he blameth not me for sin.

And in these words I saw a marvellous high privity hid in God, which privity he shall openly make known to us in Heaven: in which knowing we shall verily see the cause why he suffered sin to come. In which sight we shall endlessly joy in our Lord God.

[1] i.e., the truth.          [2] i.e., contrary to nature.

## THE TWENTY-EIGHTH CHAPTER

How the children of salvation shall be shaken in sorrows, but Christ rejoiceth with compassion; a remedy against tribulation

THUS I saw how Christ hath compassion on us for the cause of sin. And right as I was afore—in the [Shewing of the] Passion of Christ—fulfilled with pain and compassion, like so in this [sight] I was fulfilled, in part, with compassion of all mine even-Christians—for that well, well beloved people that shall be saved. For God's servants, Holy Church, shall be shaken in sorrow and anguish [and] tribulation in this world, as men shake a cloth in the wind.

And as to this our Lord answered in this manner: "A great thing shall I make thereof in Heaven of endless worship and everlasting joys."

Yea, so far forth I saw, that our Lord joyeth of the tribulations of His servants, with ruth and compassion. On each person that he loveth, to his bliss for to bring [them], he layeth something that is no lack in his sight, whereby they are blamed[1] and despised in this world, scorned, mocked, and outcasten.[2] And this he doeth for to let the harm that they should take from the pomp and the vain-glory of this wretched life, and make their way ready to come to Heaven, and up-raise[3] them in his bliss everlasting. For he saith: "I shall wholly break you of your vain affections and your vicious pride; and after that I shall together gather you, and make you mild and meek, clean and holy, by oneing to me."

And then I saw that each kind compassion that man hath on his even-Christians with charity, it is Christ in him.

[1] MS. "lakid".

[2] MS. "something that is no lak in his syte, whereby thei are lakid & dispisyd in thys world, scornyd, mokyd, & outcasten."

[3] MS. "heynen".

That same naughting that was shewed in his Passion, it was shewed again here in this Compassion. Wherein were two manner of understandings in our Lord's meaning. The one was the bliss that we are brought to, wherein he will be enjoyed. The other is for comfort in our pain: for he willeth that we wot that it shall all be turned to worship and profit by virtue of his passion, that we wot that we suffer not alone but with him, and see him [to be] our Ground, and that we see his pains and his naughting passeth so far all that we may suffer, that it may not be fully thought.

The beholding of this will save us from grudging[1] and despair in the feeling of our pains. And if we see soothly that our sin deserveth it, yet his love excuseth us, and of his great courtesy he doth away all our blame, and he holdeth us with ruth and pity as children innocent and unloathful.


## THE TWENTY-NINTH CHAPTER

Adam's sin was greatest, but the satisfaction for it is
   more pleasing to God than ever was the sin harmful

But in this I stood beholding generally, troublously and mourning, saying thus to our Lord in my meaning, with full great dread: "Ah! good Lord, how might all be well, for the great hurt that is come, by sin, to thy creatures?" And here I desired, as far as I durst, to have some more open declaring wherewith I might be eased in this [matter].

And to this our blessed Lord answered full meekly and with full lovely cheer, and shewed that Adam's sin was the most harm that ever was done, or ever shall be, to the world's end; and also he shewed that this [sin] is openly known in all Holy Church on earth. Furthermore he taught

[1] MS. "gruching", i.e., grudging, or murmuring.

that I should behold the glorious Satisfaction:[1] for this
Amends-making[2] is more pleasing to God and more worshipful, without comparison, than ever was the sin of Adam
harmful. Then meaneth our blessed Lord thus in this teaching, that we should take heed to this: "For since I have made
well the most harm, then it is my will that thou know
thereby that I shall make well all that is less."


## THE THIRTIETH CHAPTER

### How we should joy and trust in our Saviour, Jesus; not presuming to know his privy counsel

HE gave me understanding of two parts [of truth]. The one
part is our Saviour and our salvation. This blessed part is
open and clear and fair and light and plenteous,—for all
mankind that is of good will, and shall be, is comprehended
in this part. Hereto are we bounden of God, and drawn and
counselled and learned inwardly by the Holy Ghost and outwardly by Holy Church in the same grace. In this willeth our
Lord that we be occupied, joying in him; for he joyeth in
us. The more plenteously that we take of this, with reverence and meekness, the more thanks we earn[3] of him and
the more speed[4] to ourselves, thus—may we say—enjoying
our part of our Lord. The other [part] is hid and shut up
from us: that is to say, all that is beside our salvation. For it
is our Lord's privy counsel, and it belongeth to the royal
lordship of God to have his privy counsel in peace, and it
belongeth to his servant, for obedience and reverence, not

[1] MS. "asyeth".

[2] MS. "asyeth making", i.e., satisfying, atonement.

[3] MS. "deserve".          [4] i.e., profit.

to learn wholly his counsel.[1] Our Lord hath pity and compassion on us for that some creatures make themselves so busy therein; and I am sure if we wist how much we should please him and ease ourselves by leaving it, we would. The saints that be in Heaven, they will to wit nothing but that which our Lord will shew them: and also their charity and their desire is ruled after the will of our Lord: and thus ought we to will, like to them. Then shall we nothing will nor desire but the will of our Lord, as they do: for we are all one in God's meaning.

And here was I learned that we shall trust and rejoice only in our Saviour, blissful Jesus, for all thing.


## THE THIRTY-FIRST CHAPTER

Of the longing and the ghostly thirst of Christ, which lasteth and shall last till Doomsday; and by reason of his body he is not yet fully glorified, nor all impassible

AND thus our good Lord answered to all the questions and doubts that I might make, saying full comfortably: "I may make all thing well, I can make all thing well, I will make all thing well, and I shall make all thing well; and thou shalt see thyself that all manner of thing shall be well."

In that he saith, "I may," I understand [it] for the Father; and in that he saith, "I can," I understand [it] for the Son; and where he saith, "I will," I understand [it] for the Holy Ghost; and where he saith, "I shall," I understand [it] for the unity of the blessed Trinity: three Persons and one Truth;

[1] MS. "it longyth to the ryal Lordship of God to have his privy councell in pece, and it longyth to his servant for obedience and reverens not to wel wetyn his counselye".

and where he saith, "Thou shalt see thyself," I understand
the oneing of all mankind that shall be saved unto the blessed
Trinity. And in these five words God willeth we be enclosed
in rest and in peace.

Thus shall the ghostly Thirst of Christ have an end. For
this is the ghostly Thirst of Christ: the love-longing that
lasteth and ever shall, till we see that sight on Doomsday.
For we that shall be saved and shall be Christ's joy and his
bliss, some be yet here and some be to come, and so shall
some be, unto that day. Therefore this is his thirst and love-
longing, to have us altogether whole in him, to his bliss,—
as to my sight. For we be not now as fully whole in him as
we shall be then.

For we know in our Faith, and also it was shewed in all
[the Shewings] that Christ Jesus is both God and man. And
anent the Godhead, he is himself highest bliss, and was,
from without beginning, and shall be, without end: which
endless bliss may never be heightened nor lowered in itself.
For this was plenteously seen in every Shewing, and specially
in the Twelfth, where he saith: "I am that [which] is highest."
And anent Christ's Manhood, it is known in our Faith, and
also [it was] shewed, that he, with the virtue of Godhead, for
love, to bring us to his bliss, suffered pains and passions and
died. And these be the works of Christ's Manhood wherein
he rejoiceth; and that shewed he in the Ninth Shewing,
where he saith: "It is a joy and bliss and endless pleasing to
me that ever I suffered Passion for thee." And this is the bliss
of Christ's works, and thus he meaneth where he saith in
that same Shewing: we be his bliss, we be his meed, we be
his worship, we be his crown.

For anent that Christ is our Head, he is glorified and impassible; and anent his Body in which all his members be
knit, he is not yet fully glorified nor all impassible. Therefore the same desire and thirst that he had upon the Cross

(which desire, longing, and thirst, as to my sight, was in him from without beginning) the same hath he yet, and shall [have] unto the time that the last soul that shall be saved is come up to his bliss.

For as verily as there is a property in God of ruth and pity, so verily there is a property in God of thirst and longing. (And of the virtue of this longing in Christ, we have to long again to Him: without which no soul cometh to Heaven.) And this property of longing and thirst cometh of the end-less Goodness of God, right as the property of pity cometh of his endless Goodness. And though longing and pity are two sundry properties, as to my sight, in this standeth the point of the ghostly Thirst: which is lasting in him as long as we be in need, drawing us up to his bliss. And all this was seen in the Shewing of Compassion: for that shall cease on Doomsday.

Thus he hath ruth and compassion on us, and he hath longing to have us; but his wisdom and his love suffereth not the end to come till the best time.

## THE THIRTY-SECOND CHAPTER

How all things shall be well, and Scripture fulfilled, and we must steadfastly hold us in the Faith of Holy Church, as is Christ's will

ONE time our good Lord said: "All thing shall be well;" and another time he said: "Thou shalt see thyself that all *manner* thing shall be well;" and in these two [sayings] the soul took sundry understandings.

One was that he willeth we wit that not only he taketh heed to noble things and to great, but also to little and to small, to low and to simple, to one and to other. And so meaneth he in that he saith: "All manner of thing shall be well." For he willeth we wit that the least thing shall not be forgotten.

Another understanding is this, that there be deeds evil done in our sight and so great harms taken, that it seemeth to us that it were impossible that ever it should come to good end. And upon this we look, sorrowing and mourning therefor, so that we cannot resign us unto the blissful beholding of God as we should do. And the cause of this is that the use of our reason is now so blind, so low, and so simple, that we cannot know that high marvellous Wisdom, the Might and the Goodness of the blissful Trinity. And thus meaneth he when he saith: "Thou shalt see thyself that all manner of thing shall be well." As if he said: "Take now heed faithfully and trustingly, and at the last end thou shalt verily see it in fulness of joy."

And thus in these same five words aforesaid: "I may make all thing well," etc., I understand a mighty comfort of all the works of our Lord God that are yet to come. There is a Deed the which the blessed Trinity shall do in the last Day, as to my sight, and when the Deed shall be, and how it shall be done, is unknown of all creatures that are beneath Christ, and shall be till when it is done.

[1 The Goodness and the Love of our Lord God willeth that we wit that it shall be. And the Might and the Wisdom of him by the same Love will hide it, and hide from us what it shall be, and how it shall be done.]

And the cause why he willeth that we know [this Deed shall be], is for that he would have us to be the more eased in our soul and [the more] peaced in love—leaving the beholding of all tempests that might let us from true enjoying

1 This paragraph, which is missing from the Sloane MS., is here inserted from Serenus Cressy's version.

of him. This is that Great Deed ordained of our Lord God from without beginning, treasured and hid in his blessed breast, only known to himself: by which Deed he shall make all things well.

For like as the blissful Trinity made all things of naught, right so the same blessed Trinity shall make well all that is not well.

And in this sight I marvelled greatly and beheld our Faith, marvelling thus: Our Faith is grounded in God's word, and it belongeth to our Faith that we believe that God's word shall be saved in all things; and one point of our Faith is that many creatures shall be damned: as angels that fell out of Heaven for pride, which be now fiends; and man[1] in earth that dieth out of the Faith of Holy Church: that is to say, they that be heathen men; and also man[1] that hath received christendom and liveth unchristian life and so dieth out of charity: all these shall be damned to hell without end, as Holy Church teacheth me to believe. And all this [so] standing,[2] methought it was impossible that all manner of things should be well, as our Lord shewed in this time.

And as to this I had no other answer in Shewing of our Lord God but this: "That which is impossible to thee is not impossible to me: I shall save my word in all things and I shall make all things well." This I was taught, by the grace of God, that I should steadfastly hold me in the Faith as I had aforehand understood, [and] therewith that I should firmly believe[3] that all things shall be well, as our Lord shewed in the same time.

For this is the Great Deed that our Lord shall do, in which Deed he shall save his word in all thing and he shall make all well that is not well. How it shall be done there is no crea-

---

[1] Cressy, "many".　　　[2] MS. "stondyng al this".
[3] MS. "sadly levyn".

ture beneath Christ that wotteth it, nor shall wit it till it is done; according to the understanding that I took of our Lord's meaning in this time.[1]


## THE THIRTY-THIRD CHAPTER

All damned souls be despised in God's sight, as the devils. These Revelations withdraw not the Faith of Holy Church, but comfort; and the more we busy [ourselves] to know God's secrets, the less we know

AND yet in this I desired, as [far as] I durst, that I might have full sight of Hell and Purgatory. But it was not my meaning to make proof of anything that belongeth to the Faith: for I believed soothfastly that Hell and Purgatory is for the same end that Holy Church teacheth, but my meaning was that I might have seen, for learning in all things that belong to my Faith: whereby I might live the more to God's worship and to my profit.

But for [all] my desire, I could[2] [see] of this right naught, save as it is aforesaid in the First Shewing, where I saw that the devil is reproved of God and endlessly condemned. In which sight I understood as to all creatures that are of the devil's condition in this life, and therein end, that there is no more mention made of them afore God and all his Holy than of the devil,—notwithstanding that they be of mankind —whether they have been christened or not.

For though the Revelation was shewed of goodness in which was made little mention of evil, yet I was not drawn thereby from any point of the Faith that Holy Church teacheth me to believe. For I had sight of the Passion of Christ in diverse Shewings,—the First, the Second, the

[1] See Note 3, infra, p. 171.      [2] MS. "I coude of this right nowte."

Fifth, and the Eighth, as is said afore—wherein I had in part a feeling that saw him in pain; but I saw not so properly specified the Jews that did him to death. Notwithstanding I knew in my Faith that they were accursed and damned without end, saving those that [were] converted by grace. And I was strengthened and taught generally to keep me in the Faith in every point, and in all as I had before understood: hoping that I was therein with the mercy and the grace of God; desiring and praying in my meaning that I might continue therein unto my life's end.

And it is God's will that we have great regard to all his deeds that he hath done, but evermore it needeth us to leave the beholding what the Deed shall be. And desire we to be like our brethren which be saints in Heaven, that will right naught but God's will, then shall we only have joy in God and be well pleased both with hiding and with shewing. For I saw soothly in our Lord's meaning, the more we busy us to know his privities in this or any other thing, the farther shall we be from the knowing thereof.


## THE THIRTY-FOURTH CHAPTER

God sheweth the privities necessary to his lovers; and how they please God much that receive diligently the preaching of Holy Church

OUR Lord God shewed two manner of privities. One is this great privity with all the privy points that belong thereto: and these privities he willeth we should know [as] hid until the time that he will clearly shew them to us. The other are the privities that he willeth to make open and known to us; for he willeth that we wit that it is his will that we should know them. They are privities to us not only for that he willeth that they be privities to us, but they are privities to us for our blindness and our unknowing; and thereof he hath great ruth, and therefore he will himself make them more open to us, whereby we may know him and love him and cleave to him. For all that is speedful for us to wit and to know, full courteously will our Lord shew us: and [of] that is this [Shewing], with all the preaching and teaching of Holy Church.

God shewed full great pleasance that he hath in all men and women that mightily and meekly and wilfully take the preaching and teaching of Holy Church. For it is his Holy Church: he is the Ground, he is the Substance, he is the Teaching, he is the Teacher, he is the End, he is the Meed for which every kind soul travaileth.

And this [of the Shewing] is [made] known, and shall be known to every soul to which the Holy Ghost declareth it. And I hope soothly that all those that seek this, he shall speed: for they seek God.

All this that I have now said, and more that I shall say after, is comforting against sin. For in the Third Shewing when I saw that God doeth all that is done, I saw no sin: and then saw I that all is well. But when God shewed me for sin, then said he: "All shall be well."

## THE THIRTY-FIFTH CHAPTER

How God doth all that is good, and suffereth all worshipfully by his mercy, the which shall shine when sin is no longer suffered

AND when God Almighty had shewed so plenteously and so fully of his Goodness, I desired to wit of a certain creature that I loved, if it should continue in good living, which I hoped by the grace of God was begun. And in this singular desire it seemed that I letted myself: for I was not taught in this time. And then was I answered in my reason, as it were by a friendly mean:[1] "Take it *generally*, and behold the courtesy of the Lord God as he sheweth to thee: for it is more worship to God to behold him in all than in any special thing." I assented and therewith I learned that it is more worship to God to know all thing in general, than to take pleasure in any special thing.[2] And if I should do wisely after this teaching, I should not only be glad for nothing in special, but I should not be greatly dis-eased for no manner of thing: for "All shall be well." For the fulness of joy is to behold God in all: for by the same blessed Might, Wisdom, and Love, that he made all thing, to the same end our good Lord leadeth it continually, and thereto himself shall bring it; and when it is time we shall see it. And the ground of this was shewed in the First [Revelation], and more openly in the Third, where it saith: "I saw God in a point."

All that our Lord doeth is rightful, and that which he suffereth[3] is worshipful: and in these two is comprehended good and ill: for all that is good our Lord doeth, and that which is evil our Lord suffereth. I say not that any evil is worshipful, but I say the sufferance of our Lord God is worshipful: whereby his Goodness shall be known, without end, in his marvellous meekness and mildness, by the working of mercy and grace.

Rightfulness is that thing that is so good that [it] may not be better than it is. For God himself is very Rightfulness and all his works are done rightfully as they are ordained from without beginning by his high Might, his high Wisdom, his high Goodness. And right as he ordained unto the best, right so he worketh continually, and leadeth it to the same end;

---

[1] MS. "a friendful mene", i.e., intermediary, medium.
[2] MS. "than to lyken anything in special".     [3] i.e., permitteth.

and he is ever full-pleased with himself and with all his works. And the beholding of this blissful accord is full sweet to the soul that seeth by grace. All the souls that shall be saved in Heaven without end be made rightful in the sight of God, and by his own goodness: in which rightfulness we are endlessly kept, and marvellously, above all creatures.

And Mercy is a working that cometh of the goodness of God, and it shall last in working all along, as sin is suffered to pursue rightful souls. And when sin hath no longer leave to pursue, then shall the working of mercy cease, and then shall all be brought to rightfulness and therein stand without end.

And by his sufferance we fall; and in his blissful Love with his Might and his Wisdom we are kept; and by mercy and grace we are raised to manifold more joys.

Thus in Rightfulness and Mercy he willeth to be known and loved, now and without end. And the soul that wisely beholdeth it in grace, it is well pleased with both, and endlessly enjoyeth.

## THE THIRTY-SIXTH CHAPTER

Of another excellent deed our Lord shall do, which, by grace, may be learned in part here; and how we should joy in the same, and how God yet doeth miracles

OUR Lord God shewed that a deed shall be done, and himself shall do it, and I shall do nothing but sin, and my sin shall not let his Goodness [from] working. And I saw that the beholding of this is a heavenly joy in a dread full soul which evermore kindly by grace desireth God's will. This deed shall be begun here, and it shall be worshipful to God and plenteously profitable to his lovers in earth; and ever as we come to heaven we shall see it in marvellous joy, and it shall last thus in working unto the last Day; and the worship and the bliss of it shall last in Heaven afore God and all his Holy [ones] without end.

Thus was this deed seen and understood in our Lord's meaning: and the cause why he shewed it is to make us rejoice in him and in all his works. When I saw his Shewing continued, I understood that it was shewed for a great thing that was for to come, which thing God shewed that he himself should do it: which deed hath these properties aforesaid. And this shewed he well blissfully, meaning that I should take it myself wisely, faithfully, and trustingly.

But what this deed should be was kept privy from me.

And in this I saw that he willeth not [that] we dread to know the things that he sheweth. He sheweth them because he would have us know them. By which knowing he would have us love him and liken, and endlessly enjoy in him. For the great love that he hath to us he sheweth us all that is worshipful and profitable for the time. And the things that he will now have privy, yet of his great goodness he sheweth them close: in which shewing he willeth that we believe and understand that we shall see the same verily in his endless bliss. Then ought we to rejoice in him for all that he sheweth and all that he hideth; and if we wilfully and meekly do thus, we shall find therein great ease; and endless thanks we shall have of him therefor.

And this is the understanding of this word:—That it shall be done for me, [meaneth that] it is [for] the general Man: that is to say, all that shall be saved. It shall be worshipful and marvellous and plenteous, and God himself shall do it; and this shall be the highest joy that may be, to behold the deed that God himself shall do, and man shall do right naught but sin. Then meaneth our Lord God thus, as if he said: "Behold and see! Here hast thou matter of meekness, here hast thou matter of love, here hast thou matter to

63

naughten thyself, here hast thou matter to enjoy in me;—
and, for my love, enjoy [thou] in me: for of all things, therewith mightest thou most please me."

And as long as we are in this life, what time that we by
our folly turn us to the beholding of the reproved, tenderly
our Lord God toucheth us and blissfully calleth us, saying
in our soul: "Let be all thy love, my dearworthy child. Intend to me—I am enough to thee—and joy in thy Saviour
and in thy salvation." And that this is our Lord's working in
us I am sure the soul that hath understanding[1] therein by
grace shall see it and feel it.

And though it be so that this deed be truly taken for the
general Man, yet it excludeth not the special. For what our
good Lord will do by his poor creatures, it is now unknown
to me.

But this deed and that other aforesaid, they are not both
one but two sundry. This deed shall be done sooner (and
that [time] shall be as we come to Heaven), and to whom
our Lord giveth it, it may be known here in part. But that
Great Deed aforesaid shall neither be known in Heaven nor
earth till it is done.

And moreover he gave special understanding and teaching of working of miracles, as thus:—"It is known that I
have done miracles here afore, many and fell, high and
marvellous, worshipful and great. And so as I have done, I
do now continually, and shall do in coming of time."

It is known that afore miracles come sorrow and anguish
and tribulation; and that is for that we should know our own
feebleness and our mischiefs that we be fallen in by sin, to
meeken us and make us to dread God, crying for help and
grace. Miracles come after that, and they come of the high
Might, Wisdom, and Goodness of God, shewing his virtue
and the joys of Heaven so far as it may be in this passing life:

[1] MS. "is a perceyvid", i.e., has perception of it.

and that for to strengthen our faith and to increase our hope, in charity. Wherefore it pleaseth him to be known and worshipped in miracles. Then meaneth he thus: he willeth that we be not borne over low for sorrow and tempests that fall to us: for it hath ever so been afore miracle-coming.

## THE THIRTY-SEVENTH CHAPTER

God keepeth his chosen full securely, although they sin; for that in these is a godly will, that never assenteth to sin

GOD brought to my mind that I should sin. And for liking that I had in beholding of him, I attended not readily to that shewing; and our Lord full mercifully abode, and gave me grace to attend. And this shewing I took singularly to myself; but by all the gracious comfort that followeth, as ye shall see, I was learned to take it for all mine even-Christians: all in general and nothing in special: though our Lord shewed me that I should sin, by me alone is understood all.

And therein I conceived a soft dread. And to this our Lord answered: "I keep thee full surely." This word was said with more love and secureness and ghostly keeping than I can or may tell. For as it was shewed that I should sin, right so was the comfort shewed: secureness and keeping for all mine even-Christians.

What may make me more to love mine even-Christians than to see in God that he loveth all that shall be saved as it were all one soul?

For in every soul that shall be saved is a Godly Will that never assented to sin, nor ever shall. Right as there is a beastly will in the lower part that may will no good, right so there is a Godly Will in the higher part, which will is so

65

good that it may never will ill, but ever good. And therefore we are that which he loveth, and endlessly we do that which him pleaseth.

This shewed our Lord in [shewing] the wholeness of love that we stand in, in his sight: yea, that he loveth us now as well while we are here, as he shall do while we are there afore his blessed face. But for failing of love on our part, therefore is all our travail.[1]

## THE THIRTY-EIGHTH CHAPTER

Sins of the chosen shall be turned to joy and worship. Examples of David, St Peter, and St John of Beverley

ALSO God shewed that sin shall be no shame to man, but worship. For right as to every sin is answering a pain by truth, right so for every sin, to the same soul is given a bliss by love: right as diverse sins are punished with diverse pains after that they be grievous,[2] right so shall they be rewarded with diverse joys in Heaven after that they have been painful and sorrowful to the soul in earth. For the soul that shall come to Heaven is precious to God, and the place so worshipful that the goodness of God suffereth never that soul to sin that shall come there but which sin shall be rewarded; and it is made known without end, and blissfully restored by overpassing worship.

For in this Sight mine understanding was lifted up into Heaven, and then God brought merrily to my mind David, and others in the Old Law without number; and in the New Law he brought to my mind first Mary Magdalene, Peter and Paul, and those of Inde;[3] and Saint John of Beverley; and others also without number: how they are known in the

---

[1] See Note 4, *infra*, p. 174; also Introduction, p. xxiii f.

[2] i.e., according to their gravity.          [3] St Thomas and St Jude.

Church in earth with their sins, and it is to them no shame, but all is turned for them to worship. And therefore our courteous Lord sheweth for them here in part like as it is there in fulness: for there the token of sin is turned to worship.

And Saint John of Beverley, our Lord shewed him full highly, in comfort to us for homeliness; and brought to my mind how he is a kind neighbour, and of our knowing. And God called him "Saint John of Beverley" plainly as we do, and that with a full glad sweet cheer, shewing that he is a full high saint in Heaven in his sight, and a blissful. And with this he made mention that in his youth and in his tender age he was a dearworthy servant to God, greatly God loving and dreading, and yet God suffered him to fall, him mercifully keeping that he perished not, nor lost no time. And afterward God raised him to manifold more grace, and by the contrition and meekness that he had in his living, God hath given him in Heaven manifold joys, overpassing that he should have had if he had not fallen. And that this is sooth, God sheweth in earth with plenteous miracles doing about his body continually.

And all this was to make us glad and merry in love.

## THE THIRTY-NINTH CHAPTER

Of the sharpness of sin and the goodness of contrition; and how our kind Lord willeth not that we despair for often falling

SIN is the sharpest scourge that any chosen soul may be smitten with: which scourge all forbeateth man and woman, and maketh him noisome[1] in his own sight, so far forth that afterwhile[2] he thinketh himself he is not worthy but

[1] MS. "and noyith him".        [2] MS. "otherwhile".

as to sink in hell,—till [that time] when contrition forceth him by touching of the Holy Ghost, and turneth the bitterness in hopes of God's mercy. And then he beginneth his wounds to heal, and the soul to quicken [as it is] turned unto the life of Holy Church. The Holy Ghost leadeth him to confession, wilfully to shew his sins nakedly and truly, with great sorrow and great shame that he hath defouled the fair image of God. Then undergoeth he penance for every sin [as] enjoined by his doomsman[1] that is grounded in Holy Church by the teaching of the Holy Ghost. And this is one meekness that greatly pleaseth God; and also bodily sickness of God's sending, and also sorrow and shame from without, and reproof, and despite of this world, with all manner of grievance and temptations that [he] will be cast in, bodily and ghostly.

Full preciously our Lord keepeth us when it seemeth to us that we are near forsaken and cast away for our sin and because we have deserved it. And because of meekness that we get hereby, we are raised well-high in God's sight by his grace, with so great contrition, also with compassion and true longing to God. Then they be suddenly delivered from sin and from pain, and taken up to bliss, and made even high saints.

By contrition we are made clean, by compassion we are made ready, and by true longing to God we are made worthy. These are three means, as I understand, whereby that all souls come to heaven: that is to say, that have been sinners in earth and shall be saved: for by these medicines [it] behoveth that every soul be healed. Though [the soul] be healed, his wounds are seen afore God,—not as wounds but as worships. And so on the contrary-wise, as we be punished here with sorrow and with penance, we shall be rewarded in heaven by the courteous love of our Lord God

[1] i.e., Confessor.

Almighty, who willeth that none that come there lose his travail in any degree. For he [be]holdeth sin as sorrow and pain to his lovers, to whom he assigneth no blame, for love. The meed that we shall receive[1] shall not be little, but it shall be high, glorious, and worshipful. And so shall shame be turned to worship and more joy.

But our courteous Lord willeth not that his servants despair, for often nor for grievous falling: for our falling letteth not him from loving us. Peace and love are ever in us, being and working; but we be not always in peace and in love. But he willeth that we take heed thus that he is Ground of all our whole life in love; and furthermore that he is our everlasting Keeper and mightily defendeth us against our enemies, that be full fell and fierce upon us;— and so much our need is the more for [that] we give them occasion by our falling.


## THE FORTIETH CHAPTER

The vileness of sin passeth all pains, and God loveth us well tenderly while we be in sin, and so us needeth to love our neighbour

THIS is a sovereign friendship of our courteous Lord that he keepeth us so tenderly while we be in sin; and furthermore he toucheth us full privily and sheweth us our sin by the sweet light of mercy and grace. But when we see our self so foul, then ween we that God were wroth with us for our sin, and then are we stirred of the Holy Ghost by contrition unto prayer and desire for the amending of our life with all our mights, to slake the wrath of God, unto the time we find a rest in soul and a softness in conscience. Then hope

[1] MS. "underforgyn".

we that God hath forgiven us our sins: and it is sooth. And then sheweth our courteous Lord himself to the soul—well-merrily and with glad cheer—with friendful welcoming as if it[1] had been in pain and in prison, saying sweetly thus: "My darling, I am glad thou art come to me: in all thy woe I have ever been with thee; and now seest thou my loving and we be oned in bliss." Thus are sins forgiven by mercy and grace, and our soul [is] worshipfully received in joy, like as it shall be when it cometh to Heaven, as oftentimes as it cometh by the gracious working of the Holy Ghost and the virtue of Christ's Passion.

Here understand I soothly that all manner of things are made ready for us by the great goodness of God, so far forth that, what time we be ourselves in peace and charity, we be verily saved. But because we may not have this in fulness while we are here, therefore it falleth to us evermore to live in sweet prayer and lovely longing with our Lord Jesus. For he longeth ever to bring us to the fulness of joy; as it is aforesaid, where he sheweth the ghostly Thirst.

But now if any man or woman, because of all this ghostly comfort that is aforesaid, be stirred by folly to say or to think: "If this be sooth, then were it good to sin [so as] to have the more meed,"—or else to charge the less [guilt] to sin,—beware of this stirring: for soothly if it come it is untrue, and of the enemy of the same true love that teacheth us all this comfort. The same blessed Love teacheth us that we should hate sin only for love. I am sure by mine own feeling, the more that every kind soul seeth this in the courteous love of our Lord God, the lother he is to sin and the more he is ashamed. For if afore us were laid all the pains in Hell and in Purgatory and in Earth—death and other— [on the one hand] and sin [on the other], we should rather choose all that pain than sin. For sin is so vile and so greatly

[1] MS. "he", i.e., the soul.

to be hated that it may be likened to no pain which is not sin. And to me was shewed no harder hell than sin. For a kind soul hath no hell but sin.

And [when] we give our intent to love and meekness, by the working of mercy and grace we are made all fair and clean. As mighty and as wise as God is to save men, so willing he is. For Christ himself is [the] ground of all the laws of Christian men, and he taught us to do good against ill: here may we see that he is himself this charity, and doeth to us as he teacheth us to do. For he willeth that we be like him in wholeness of endless love to ourself and to our even-Christians: no more than his love is broken to us for our sin, no more willeth he that our love be broken to ourself and to our even-Christians: but [that we] nakedly hate the sin and endlessly love the soul, as God loveth it. Then shall we hate sin like as God hateth it, and love the soul as God loveth it. And this word that he said is an endless comfort: "I keep thee securely."

## THE FORTY-FIRST CHAPTER

The Fourteenth Revelation is as aforesaid; how it is impossible we should pray for mercy and want it: and how God willeth we pray alway, though we be dry and barren, for that prayer is to him acceptable and pleasant

AFTER this our Lord shewed concerning Prayer. In which shewing I see two conditions in our Lord's meaning: one is rightfulness, another is sure trust.

But yet oftentimes our trust is not full: for we are not sure that God heareth us, as we think because of our unworthiness, and because we feel right naught—for we are as barren and dry oftentimes after our prayers as we were afore; and this, in our feeling our folly, is cause of our weakness.[1] For thus have I felt in myself.

And all this brought our Lord suddenly to my mind, and shewed these words, and said: "I am Ground of thy beseeching: first it is my will that thou have it; and after, I make thee to will it; and since, I make thee to beseech it and thou beseechest it, how should it then be that thou shouldst not have thy beseeching?"

And thus in the first reason, with the three that follow, our good Lord sheweth a mighty comfort, as it may be seen in the same words. And in the first reason,—where he saith: "And thou beseechest it," there he sheweth [his] full great pleasance, and endless meed that he will give us for our beseeching. And in the second reason, where he saith: "How should it then be?" etc., this was said for an impossible [thing]. For it is most impossible that we should beseech mercy and grace, and not have it. For everything that our good Lord maketh us to beseech, himself hath ordained it to us from without beginning. Here may we see that our beseeching is not cause of God's goodness; and that shewed he soothfastly in all these sweet words when he saith: "I am [the] Ground."—And our good Lord willeth that this be known of his lovers in earth; and the more that we know [it] the more should we beseech, if it be wisely taken; and so is our Lord's meaning.

Beseeching is a new, gracious, lasting will of the soul, oned and fastened into the will of our Lord by the sweet inward work of the Holy Ghost. Our Lord himself, he is the first receiver of our prayer, as to my sight, and taketh it full thankfully and highly enjoying; and he sendeth it up above and setteth it in the Treasure, where it shall never perish. It is there afore God with all his Holy continually received, ever speeding [the help of] our needs; and when we shall

[1] MS. "And this in our felyng our foly is cause of our wekenes."

receive our bliss it shall be given us for a degree of joy, with endless worshipful thanking of him.

Full glad and merry is our Lord of our prayer; and he looketh thereafter and he will have it because with his grace he maketh us like to himself in condition as we are in kind: and so is his blissful will. Therefore he saith thus: "Pray inwardly,[1] though thee thinketh it savour thee not: for it is profitable, though thou feel not, though thou see naught; yea, though thou think thou mayst naught. For in dryness and in barrenness, in sickness and in feebleness, then is thy prayer well-pleasant to me, though thee thinketh it savour thee naught but little. And so is all thy believing prayer in my sight." For the meed and the endless thanks that he will give us, therefore he is covetous to have us pray continually in his sight. God accepteth the good-will and the travail of his servant, howsoever we feel: wherefore it pleaseth him that we work both in our prayers and in good living, by his help and his grace, reasonably with discretion keeping our mights[2] [turned] to him, till when that we have him that we seek, in fulness of joy: that is, Jesus. And that shewed he in the Fifteenth [Revelation], farther on, in this word: "Thou shalt have me to thy meed."

And also to prayer belongeth thanking. Thanking is a true inward knowing, with great reverence and lovely dread turning ourselves with all our mights unto the working that our good Lord stirreth us to, enjoying and thanking inwardly. And sometimes, for plenteousness it breaketh out with voice, and saith "Good Lord, Grant mercy! Blessed mayst thou be!" And sometime when the heart is dry and feeleth not, or else by temptation of our enemy,—then it is driven by reason and by grace to cry upon our Lord with voice, rehearsing his blessed Passion and his great Goodness; and the virtue of our Lord's word turneth into the soul and quicken-

[1] MS. "inderly".    [2] i.e., faculties.

eth the heart and entereth[1] it by his grace into true working, and maketh it pray right blissfully. And truly to enjoy our Lord, it is a full blissful thanking in his sight.

## THE FORTY-SECOND CHAPTER

Of three things that belong to prayer: How we should pray. Of the goodness of God that supplieth always our imperfections and feebleness when we do that which belongeth to us to do

OUR Lord God willeth [that] we have true understanding, and specially in three things that belong to our prayer. The first is by whom and how that our prayer springeth. By whom, he sheweth when he saith: "I am [the] Ground;" and how, by his Goodness: for he saith first: "It is my will." The second is: in what manner and how we should use our prayer; and that is that our will be turned unto the will of our Lord, enjoying: and so meaneth he when he saith: "I make thee to will it." The third is that we should know the fruit and the end of our prayers: that is, that we be oned and like to our Lord in all things; and to this intent and for this end was all this lovely lesson shewed. And he will help us, and we shall make it so as he saith himself;—Blessed may he be!

For this is our Lord's will, that our prayer and our trust be both alike large. For if we trust not as much as we pray, we do not full worship to our Lord in our prayer, and also we tarry[2] and pain our self. The cause is, as I believe, that we know not truly that our Lord is [the] Ground on whom our prayer springeth; and also that we know not that it is given us by the grace of his love. For if we knew this, it

[1] MS. "entrith", i.e., leadeth.     [2] i.e., tire.

would make us to trust to have, of our Lord's gift, all that
we desire. For I am sure that no man asketh mercy and
grace with true meaning, but if mercy and grace be first
given to him.

But sometimes it cometh to our mind that we have prayed
long time, and yet we think to ourselves that we have not
our asking. But herefor should we not be heavy. For I am
sure, by our Lord's meaning, that either we abide a better
time, or more grace, or a better gift. He willeth that we
have true knowing in himself that he is Being; and in this
knowing he willeth that our understanding be grounded,
with all our mights and all our intent and all our meaning;
and in this ground he willeth that we take our stand and our
oneing, and by the gracious light of himself he willeth that
we have understanding of the things that follow. The first is
our noble and excellent making; the second, our precious
and dearworthy again-buying; the third, all thing that he
hath made beneath us, [he hath made] to serve us, and for our
love keepeth it. Then meaneth he thus, as if he said: "Behold
and see that I have done all this before thy prayers; and now
thou art, and prayest me." And thus he meaneth that it belongeth to us to wit that the greatest deeds be [already] done,
as Holy Church teacheth; and in the beholding of this, with
thanking, we ought to pray for the deed that is now in doing:
and that is, that he rule and guide us, to his worship, in this
life, and bring us to his bliss. And therefor he hath done all.

Then meaneth he thus: that we [should] see that he doeth
it, and that we [should] pray therefor. For the one is not
enough. For if we pray and see not that he doeth it, it
maketh us heavy and doubtful; and that is not his worship.
And if we see that he doeth, and we pray not, we do not our
debt, and so may it not be: that is to say, so is it not [the
thing that is] in his beholding. But to see that he doeth it,
and to pray forthwithal,—so is he worshipped and we sped.

All thing that our Lord hath ordained to do, it is his will that we pray therefor, either in special or in general. And the joy and the bliss that it is to him, and the thanks and the worship that we shall have therefor, it passeth the understanding of creatures, as to my sight.

For prayer is a right wise understanding of that fulness of joy that is to come, with well-longing and sure trust. Failing of our bliss that we be kindly ordained to, maketh us for to long; and true understanding and love, with sweet mind in our Saviour, graciously maketh us to trust. And in these two workings our Lord beholdeth us continually: for it is our due part, and his Goodness may no less assign to us.

Thus it belongeth to us to do our diligence; and when we have done it, then shall us yet think that [it] is naught—and sooth it is. But if we do as we may, and soothly ask [for] mercy and grace, all that faileth us we shall find in him. And thus meaneth he where he saith: "I am Ground of thy beseeching." And thus in this blissful word, with the Shewing, I saw a full over-coming against all our weakness and all our doubtful dreads.


## THE FORTY-THIRD CHAPTER

What prayer doth when ordained to God's will; and how the goodness of God hath great liking in the deeds that he doth by us, as if he were beholden to us, working all things full sweetly

PRAYER oneth the soul to God. For though the soul be ever like to God in kind and substance, restored by grace, it is often unlike in condition, by sin on man's part. Then is prayer a witness that the soul willeth as God willeth; and it comforteth the conscience and [en]ableth man to grace.

And thus he teacheth us to pray, and mightily to trust that we shall have it. For he beholdeth us in love and would make us partners of his good deed, and therefore he stirreth us to prayer for that which it liketh him to do. For which prayer and good-will, that we have of his gift, he will reward us and give us endless meed.

And this was shewed in this word: "And thou beseechest it." In this word God shewed so great pleasance and so great liking, as [though] he were much beholden to us for every good deed that we do (and yet it is he that doth it) because that we beseech him mightily to do all thing that him liketh as if he said: "What might then please me more than to beseech [me] mightily, wisely, and earnestly, to do that thing that I shall do?"

And thus the soul by prayer accordeth to God.

But when our courteous Lord of his grace sheweth himself to our soul, we have that [which] we desire. And then we see not, for the time, what we should more pray, but all our intent with all our might is set wholly to the beholding of him. And this is an high unperceivable prayer, as to my sight: for all the cause wherefor we pray, it is oned into the sight and beholding of him to whom we pray; marvellously enjoying with reverent dread, and with so great sweetness and delight in him that we can pray right naught but as he stirreth us, for the time. And well I wot, the more the soul seeth of God, the more it desireth him by his grace.

But when we see him not so, then feel we need and cause to pray, for failing and for unabling of our self, to Jesus. For when the soul is tempested, troubled, and left to itself by unrest, then it is time to pray, for to make itself supple and buxom to God. (But the soul by no manner of prayer maketh God supple to it: for he is ever alike in love.)

And this I saw: that what time we see needs wherefor we pray, then our good Lord followeth us, helping our desire;

and when we of his special grace plainly behold him, seeing none other needs, then we follow him and he draweth us into him by love. For I saw and felt that his marvellous and fulsome Goodness fulfilleth all our might; and therewith I saw that his continual working in all manner of things is done so goodly, so wisely, and so mightily, that it over-passeth all our imagining, and all that we can ween and think; and then we can do no more but behold him, enjoy-ing, with an high, mighty desire to be all oned into him,— centred to his dwelling,[1]—and enjoy in his loving and delight in his goodness.

And then shall we, with his sweet grace, in our own meek continuant prayer come into him now in this life by many privy touchings of sweet ghostly sights and feeling, measured to us as our simpleness may bear it. And this is wrought, and shall be, by the grace of the Holy Ghost, so long till we shall die in longing, for love. And then shall we all come into our Lord, our Self clearly knowing, and God fully having; and we shall endlessly be all had in God: him verily seeing and fulsomely feeling, him ghostly hearing, and him delectably smelling, and [of] him sweetly swallowing.

And then shall we see God face to face, homely and ful-somely. The creature, that is made, shall see and endlessly behold God, which is the Maker. For thus may no man see God and live after, that is to say, in this deadly life. But when he of his special grace will shew himself here, he strengtheneth the creature above the self, and he measureth the Shewing, after his own will, as it is profitable for the time.

[1] MS. "wonyng".

## THE FORTY-FOURTH CHAPTER

Of the properties of the Trinity, and how a creature
hath the same properties, doing that which it was made
for, seeing, beholding, and marvelling at his God, so
that he seemeth to himself as naught

GOD shewed in all the Revelations, oftentimes, that man
worketh evermore his will and his worship lastingly without
any stinting. And what this work is, was shewed in the First,
and that in a marvellous example: for it was shewed in the
working of the soul of our blissful Lady Saint Mary: [that
is, the working of] Truth and Wisdom. And how [it is done]
I hope by the grace of the Holy Ghost I shall tell, as I saw.

Truth seeth God, and Wisdom beholdeth God, and of
these two cometh the third: that is, a holy marvellous
delight in God; which is Love. Where Truth and Wisdom
are verily, there is Love verily, coming of them both. And
all of God's making: for he is endless sovereign Truth, endless sovereign Wisdom, endless sovereign Love, unmade;
and man's Soul is a creature in God which hath the same
properties made and evermore it doeth that it was made for:
it seeth God, it beholdeth God, and it loveth God. Whereof
God enjoyeth in the creature; and the creature in God, endlessly marvelling.

In which marvelling he seeth his God, his Lord, his
Maker, so high, so great, and so good, in comparison with
him that is made, that scarcely[1] the creature seemeth aught
to the self. But the clarity and the clearness of Truth and
Wisdom maketh him to see and to know that he is made for
Love: in which God endlessly keepeth him.

---

[1] MS. "one thys".

## THE FORTY-FIFTH CHAPTER

### Of the deep judgement of God and the variant judgement of men .

GOD doometh us [looking] upon our kind Substance, which is ever kept one in Him, whole and safe without end: and this doom is [because] of his rightfulness [in the which it is made and kept]. And man judgeth [looking] upon our changeable Sensuality, which seemeth now one [thing], now other,—according as it taketh of the [higher or lower] parts, —and [is that which] showeth outward. And this wisdom [of man's judgement] is mingled[1] [because of the diverse things it beholdeth]. For sometimes it is good and easy, and sometimes it is hard and grievous. And in as much as it is good and easy it belongeth to the rightfulness; and in as much as it is hard and grievous, by reason of the sin beheld, which sheweth in our Sensuality, our good Lord Jesus reformeth it, by the working in our Sensuality of mercy and grace through the virtue of his blessed Passion and so bringeth [it] into the rightfulness.

And though these two [judgements] be thus accorded and oned, yet both shall be known in Heaven without end. The first doom is of God's rightfulness, and that is [because] of his high endless life in our kind Substance; and this is that fair sweet doom that was shewed in all the fair Revelation, in which I saw him assign to us no manner of blame. But though this was sweet and delectable, yet in the beholding only of this, I could not be fully eased: and that was for the doom of Holy Church, which I had afore understood and [which] was continually in my sight. And therefore by this doom methought me behoved needs to know me a sinner, and by the same doom I understood that sinners are worthy

[1] MS. "medyllid".

sometime of blame and wrath; but these two could I not see in God; and therefore my desire was more than I can or may tell. For the higher doom God shewed himself, in that same time, and therefore me behoved needs to take it; and the lower doom was learned me afore in Holy Church, and therefore I might in no way leave the lower doom. Then was this my desire: that I might see in God in what manner that [which] the doom of Holy Church teacheth is true in his sight, and how it belongeth to me soothly to know it; whereby the [two dooms] might both be saved, so as it were worshipful to God and right way to me.

And to all this I had none other answer but a marvellous example of a lord and of a servant, as I shall tell after: and that full mistily[1] shewed. And yet I stand in desire, and will unto my end, that I might by grace know these two dooms as it belongeth to me. For all heavenly, and all earthly things belonging to Heaven, are comprehended in these two dooms. And the more understanding, by the gracious leading of the Holy Ghost, that we have of these two dooms, the more we shall see and know our failings. And ever the more that we see them, the more kindly, by grace, we shall long to be fulfilled of endless joy and bliss. For we are made thereto, and our kindly Substance is now blissful in God, and hath been since it was made, and shall be without end.

[1] *Sic* in MS. See Chap. 51 et seq. The misty-ness seems to refer not to the clearness of the shewing but to the difficulty of interpreting its meaning.

## THE FORTY-SIXTH CHAPTER

We cannot know ourselves in this life but by faith and grace, but we must know ourselves sinners, and how sinful. God is never wroth, being most near the soul, it keeping

Our passing life that we have here in our sensuality knoweth not what our Self is, but then shall we verily and clearly see and know our Lord God in fulness of joy. And therefore it behoveth needs to be that the nearer we be to our bliss, the more we shall long [for it] : and that both by kind and by grace. We may have knowing of our Self in this life by continuant help and virtue of our high kind. In which knowing we may exercise and wax, by furthering and speeding of mercy and grace; but we may never fully know our Self until the last point : in which point this passing life and manner of pain and woe shall have an end. And therefore it belongeth properly to us, both by kind and by grace, to long and desire with all our mights to know our Self in fulness of endless joy.

And yet in all this time, from the beginning to the end, I had two manner of beholdings. The one was endless continuant love, with secureness of keeping, and blissful salvation, for of this was all the Shewing. The other was the common teaching of Holy Church, in which I was afore informed and grounded and wilfully have in use and understanding. And the beholding of this went not from me : for by the Shewing I was not stirred nor led therefrom in no manner of point, but I had therein teaching to love it and liken it : whereby I might, by the help of our Lord and his grace, increase and rise to more heavenly knowing and higher loving.

And thus in all the Beholding methought it behoved

needs to see and to know that we are sinners, and do many evils that we ought to leave, and leave many good deeds undone that we ought to do: wherefore we deserve pain and wrath. And notwithstanding all this, I saw soothfastly that our Lord was never wroth, nor ever shall be. For he is God: Good, Life, Truth, Love, Peace; his charity and his unity suffereth him not to be wroth. For I saw truly that it is against the property of [his] might to be wroth, and against the property of his Wisdom, and against the property of his Goodness. God is the Goodness that may not be wroth, for he is not [other] but Goodness: our soul is oned to him, unchangeable goodness, and between God and our soul is neither wrath nor forgiveness in his sight. For our soul is fulsomely oned to God of his own Goodness that betwixt God and soul may be right naught.

And to this understanding was the soul led by love and drawn by might in every Shewing: that it is thus our good Lord shewed and how it is thus soothly of his great Goodness. And he willeth that we desire to wit it—that is to say, as it belongeth to his creature to learn it—for all things that the simple soul understood, God willeth that they be shewed and known. For the things that he will have privy, mightily and wisely himself he hideth them, for love. For I saw in the same Shewing that much privity is hid, which may never be known until the time that God of his goodness hath made us worthy to see it; and therewith I am well content,[1] abiding our Lord's will in this high marvel. And now I yield me to my Mother, Holy Church, as a simple child ought.

[1] MS. "paid".

## THE FORTY-SEVENTH CHAPTER

*We must reverently marvel and meekly suffer, ever joying in God; and how our blindness, in that we see not God, is because of sin*

Two points belong to our soul by debt: the one is that we reverently marvel, the other is that we meekly suffer, ever joying in God. For he will that we wit how we shall in short time see clearly in himself all that we desire.

And notwithstanding all this, I beheld and marvelled greatly: [saying] "What is the mercy and forgiveness of God?" For by the teaching that I had afore, I understood that the mercy of God should be the forgiveness of his wrath after the time that we have sinned. For methought that to a soul whose meaning and desire is to love, the wrath of God was harder than any other pain, and therefore I took [it] that the forgiveness of his wrath should be one of the principal points of his mercy. But for all I might behold and desire, I could in no wise see this point in all the Shewing.[1]

But how I understood and saw of the works of mercy, I shall tell somewhat, as God will give me grace. I understood this: Man is changeable in this life, and by frailty and overcoming falleth into sin: he is unmighty and unwise of himself, and also his will is overlaid. And in this time he is in tempest and in sorrow and woe; and the cause is blindness: for he seeth not God. For if he saw God continually, he should have no mischievous feeling, nor any manner of stirring or yearning that serveth to sin.[2]

Thus saw I, and felt in the same time; and methought that the sight and the feeling was high and plenteous and gracious in comparison with that which our common feeling

[1] MS. "But for nowte that I myte beholden and desyrin I could not se."
[2] MS. "ne no manner steryng ne yernyng".

is in this life; but yet I thought it was but small and low in comparison with the great desire that the soul hath to see God.

For I felt in me five manner of workings, which be these:
enjoying, mourning, desire, dread, and sure hope. Enjoying: for God gave me understanding and knowing that it was
himself that I saw; mourning: and that was for failing;
desire: and that was I might see him ever more and more,
understanding and knowing that we shall never have full
rest till we see him verily and clearly in heaven; dread: was
for it seemed to me in all that time that that sight should
fail, and I be left to myself; sure hope: was in the endless
love, that I saw I should be kept by his mercy and brought
to his bliss. And the joying in his sight with this sure hope
of his merciful keeping made me to have feeling and comfort so that mourning and dread were not greatly painful.
And yet in all this I beheld in the Shewing of God that this
manner of sight of him may not be continuant in this life,—
and that for his own worship and for increase of our endless
joy. And therefore we fail oftentimes of the sight of him,
and anon we fall into our self, and then find we no feeling
of right,—naught but contrariness that is in our self; and
that of the elder root of our first sin, with all [the sins] that
follow, of our contrivance. And in this we are travailed and
tempested with feeling of sins and of pains, in many divers
manners, ghostly, and bodily, as it [is] known to us in this
life.


## THE FORTY-EIGHTH CHAPTER

Of mercy and grace and their properties; and how we
shall rejoice that ever we suffered woe patiently

BUT our good Lord the Holy Ghost, which is endless life
dwelling in our soul full securely, keepeth us, and worketh

therein a peace and bringeth it to ease by grace, and accordeth it to God and maketh it buxom. And this is the mercy and the way that our Lord continually leadeth us in as long as we be here in this life which is changeable.

For I saw no wrath but on man's part; and that forgiveth he in us. For wrath is naught else but a frowardness and a contrariness to peace and to love; and either it cometh of failing of might, or of failing of wisdom, or of failing of goodness: which failing is not in God, but it is on our part. For we by sin and wretchedness have in us a wretched and continuant contrariness to peace and to love. And that shewed he full often in his lovely cheer of Ruth and Pity. For the ground of mercy is love, and the working of mercy is our keeping in love. And this was shewed in such manner that I could[1] not have perceived of the part of mercy otherwise but as it were alone in love; that is to say, as to my sight.

Mercy is a sweet gracious working in love, mingled with plenteous pity: for mercy worketh, keeping us, and mercy worketh turning for us all things to good. Mercy, by love, suffereth us to fail in measure: and in as much as we fail, in so much we fall: and in as much as we fall, in so much we die: for it needs must be that we die in so much as we fail of the sight and feeling of God that is our life. Our failing is dreadful, our falling is shameful, and our dying is sorrowful: but in all this the sweet eye of pity and love cometh never off us, nor the working of mercy ceaseth.

For I beheld the property of mercy, and I beheld the property of grace: which have two manners of working in one love. Mercy is a pitiful property which belongeth to the Motherhood in tender love; and grace is a worshipful property which belongeth to the royal Lordship in the same love. Mercy worketh: keeping, suffering, quickening, and healing; and all is of tenderness of love. And grace worketh:

[1] MS. "I cowth not a perceyven of".

raising, rewarding, and endlessly overpassing that which our longing and our travail deserveth, spreading abroad and shewing the high plenteous largesse of God's royal Lordship in his marvellous courtesy; and this is of the abundance of love. For grace worketh our dreadful failing into plenteous, endless solace; and grace worketh our shameful falling into high, worshipful rising; and grace worketh our sorrowful dying into holy, blissful life.

For I saw full surely that ever as our contrariness worketh to us here in earth pain, shame, and sorrow, right so, on the contrary wise, grace worketh to us in heaven solace, worship, and bliss. And overpassing so far forth that, when we come up and receive the sweet reward which grace hath wrought for us, then we shall thank and bless our Lord, endlessly joying that ever we suffered woe. And that shall be for a property of blessed love that we shall know in God which we might never have known without woe going before.

And when I saw all this, it behoved me needs to grant that the mercy of God and the forgiveness is to slacken and waste our wrath.


## THE FORTY-NINTH CHAPTER

Our life is grounded in love, without the which we perish. Yet God is never wroth, but in our wrath and sin he mercifully keepeth us and treateth with us for peace, rewarding our tribulations

For this was an high marvel to the soul which was continually shewed in all [the Revelations] and with great diligence beholden, that our Lord God, anent himself may not forgive, for he may not be wroth: it were impossible. For this was shewed: that our life is all grounded and rooted in love, and without love we may not live; and therefore to the soul that of his special grace seeth so far forth the high, marvellous Goodness of God, and seeth that we are endlessly oned to him in love, it is the most impossible that may be, that God should be wroth. For wrath and friendship be two contraries. For he that wasteth and destroyeth our wrath and maketh us meek and mild,—it behoveth needs to be that he be ever one in love, meek and mild: which is contrary to wrath.

For I saw full surely that where our Lord appeareth, peace is taken and wrath hath no place. For I saw no manner of wrath in God, neither for short time nor for long;—for soothly, as to my sight, if God might be wroth for an instant, [1] we should never have life nor stay nor being. For as verily as we have our being of the endless Might of God and of the endless Wisdom and of the endless Goodness, so verily we have our keeping in the endless Might of God, in the endless Wisdom, and in the endless Goodness. For though we feel in us wretches, debates and strifes, yet are we all-mannerful enclosed in the mildness of God and in his meekness, in his benignity and in his graciousness. [2] For I saw full surely that all our endless friendship, our stay, our life, and our being, is in God.

For that same endless Goodness that keepeth us when we sin, that we perish not, the same endless Goodness continually treateth in us a peace against our wrath and our contrarious falling, and maketh us to see our need with a true dread, [and] mightily to seek unto God to have forgiveness, with a gracious desire of our salvation. And though we, by the wrath and the contrariness that is in us, be now in tribulation, disease, and woe, as falleth to our blindness and frailty, yet are we securely safe by the merciful keeping

[1] MS. "a touch".          [2] MS. "buxumhede".

of God, that we perish not. But we are not blissfully safe,
in having of our endless joy, till we be all in peace and in
love: that is to say, full pleased with God and with all his
works, and with all his dooms ,and loving and peaceable with
our self and with our even-Christians and with all that God
loveth, as love liketh. And this doeth God's Goodness in us.

Thus saw I that God is our very Peace, and he is our sure
Keeper when we are ourselves in unpeace, and he continually worketh to bring us into endless peace. And thus when
we, by the working of mercy and grace, be made meek and
mild, we are full safe; suddenly is the soul oned to God
when it is truly peaced in itself: for in him is found no
wrath. And thus I saw when we are all in peace and in love,
we find no contrariness, nor no manner of letting through
that contrariness which is now in us; [nay], our Lord of his
Goodness maketh it to us full profitable. For that contrariness is cause of our tribulations and all our woe, and our
Lord Jesus taketh them and sendeth them up to Heaven, and
there are they made more sweet and delectable than heart
may think or tongue may tell. And when we come thither
we shall find them ready, all turned into very fair and endless worships. Thus is God our steadfast Ground: and he
shall be our full bliss and make us unchangeable, as he is,
when we are there.

## THE FIFTIETH CHAPTER

How the chosen soul was never dead in the sight of God;
of a marvel upon the same; three things emboldened her
to ask God the understanding of it

AND in this deadly life mercy and forgiveness is our way
and evermore leadeth us to grace. And by the tempest and

the sorrow that we fall into on our part, we be often dead as to man's doom in earth; but in the sight of God the soul that shall be saved was never dead, nor ever shall be.

But yet here I wondered and marvelled with all the diligence of my soul, meaning thus: "Good Lord, I see thee that art very Truth; and I know that we soothly sin grievously all day and be much blameworthy; and I may neither leave the knowing of thy sooth, nor do I see thee shew to us any manner of blame. How may this be?"

For I knew by the common teaching of Holy Church and by mine own feeling, that the blame of our sin continually hangeth upon us, from the first man unto the time that we come up unto heaven: then was this my marvel that I saw our Lord God shewing to us no more blame than if we were as clean and as holy as Angels be in heaven. And betwixt these two contraries my reason was greatly travailed by my blindness, and could have no rest for dread that his blessed presence should pass from my sight and I be left in unknowing [of] how he beholdeth us in our sin. For either [it] behoved me to see in God that sin was all done away, or else me behoved to see in God how he seeth it, whereby I might truly know how it belongeth to me to see sin, and the manner of our blame. My longing endured, him continually beholding;—and yet I could have no patience for great awe and perplexity, thinking: "If I take it thus that we be not sinners and no [wise] blameworthy, it seemeth as I should err and fail of knowing of this sooth; and if it be so that we be sinners and blameworthy,—Good Lord, how may it then be that I cannot see this soothness in thee, which art my God, my Maker, in whom I desire to see all truths?"[1]

For three points make me hardy to ask it. The first is, because it is so low a thing: for if it were an high [thing] I should be a-dread. The second is, that it is so common: for

[1] MS. "Trueths".

if it were special and privy, also I should be a-dread. The
third is, that it needeth me to know it, as methinketh, if I
shall live here for knowing of good and evil, whereby I may,
by reason and grace, the more dispart them asunder, and
love goodness and hate evil, as Holy Church teacheth. I
cried inwardly, with all my might seeking unto God for
help, saying thus: "Ah! Lord Jesus, King of bliss, how shall
I be eased? Who shall teach me and tell me that [which]
me needeth to wit, if I may not at this time see it in thee?"

## THE FIFTY-FIRST CHAPTER

The answer to the doubt aforesaid, by a marvellous
example of our Lord as a servant

AND then our courteous Lord answered in shewing full
mistily a wonderful example of a Lord that hath a servant:
and he gave me sight to my understanding of both. Which
sight was shewed doubly in the Lord and doubly in the
Servant: the one part was shewed ghostly in bodily likeness,
and the other part was shewed more ghostly, without bodily
likeness.

For the first [sight], thus, I saw two persons in bodily
likeness: that is to say, a Lord and a Servant; and therewith
God gave me a ghostly understanding. The Lord sitteth
solemnly in rest and in peace; the Servant standeth by, afore
his Lord reverently, ready to do his Lord's will. The Lord
looketh upon his Servant full lovingly and sweetly, and
meekly he sendeth him to a certain place to do his will. The
Servant not only he goeth, but suddenly he starteth, and
runneth in great haste, for love to do his Lord's will. And
anon he falleth into a slade,[1] and taketh full great hurt.[2] And

[1] i.e., a steep place or ravine.          [2] MS. "sore".

then he groaneth and moaneth and waileth and writheth, but he neither may rise nor help himself by no manner of way.

And of all this the most mischief that I saw him in, was failing of comfort: for he could not turn his face to look upon his loving Lord, which was to him full near,—in whom is full comfort;—but as a man that was feeble and unwise for the time, he gave intent to his feeling and endured in woe.

In which woe he suffered seven great pains. The first was the sore bruising that he took in his falling, which was to him feelable pain; the second was the heaviness of his body; the third was feebleness following from these two; the fourth, that he was blinded in his reason and stunned in his mind, so far forth that almost he had forgotten his own love; the fifth was that he might not rise; the sixth was most marvellous to me, and that was that he lay all alone: I looked all about and beheld, and far nor near, high nor low, I saw to him no help: the seventh was that the place which he lay on was a long, hard, and grievous [one].

I marvelled how this Servant might meekly suffer there all this woe, and I beheld with carefulness[1] to learn[2] if I could perceive in him any fault, or if the Lord should assign to him any blame. And soothly there was none seen: for only his goodwill and his great desire was cause of his falling; and he was unlothful, and as good inwardly as when he stood afore his Lord, ready to do his will. And right thus continually his loving Lord full tenderly beholdeth him. But now with a double cheer: one outward, full meekly and mildly, with great ruth and pity,—and this was of the first [sight]: another inward, more ghostly,—and this was shewed with a leading of mine understanding into the Lord, [in the] which I saw him highly rejoicing for the worshipful resting and nobleness that he will and shall bring his Servant

[1] MS. "avisement".          [2] MS. "wetyn".

to by his plenteous grace; and this was of that other shewing.

And now [was] my understanding led again into the first [sight]; both keeping in mind. Then saith this courteous Lord in his meaning: "Lo, lo, my loved Servant, what harm and dis-ease he hath taken in my service for my love,—yea, and for his goodwill. Is it not fit[1] that I award him [for] his affright and his dread, his hurt and his maim and all his woe? And not only this, but falleth it not to me to give a gift that [shall] be better to him, and more worshipful, than his own wholeness should have been?—or else methinketh I should do him no grace."

And in this an inward ghostly Shewing of the Lord's meaning descended into my soul: in which I saw that it behoveth needs to be, by virtue of his great [goodness] and his own worship, that his dearworthy Servant, which he loved so much, should be verily and blissfully rewarded without end, above that he should have been if he had not fallen. Yea, and so far forth, that his falling and his woe, that he hath taken thereby, shall be turned into high and overpassing worship and endless bliss.

And at this point the shewing of the example vanished, and our good Lord led forth mine understanding in sight and in shewing of the Revelation to the end. But notwithstanding all this forth-leading, the marvelling of the example went never from me: for methought it was given me for an answer to my desire, and yet could I not take therein full understanding to mine ease at that time. For in the Servant that was shewed for Adam, as I shall say, I saw many diverse properties that might in no manner or way be assigned[2] to single Adam. And thus in that time I stood much in unknowing: for the full understanding of this marvellous example was not given me in that time. In which mighty example three properties of the Revelation be yet greatly hid; and

[1] MS. "skyl".       [2] MS. "aret", i.e., reckoned.

notwithstanding this [further explaining], I saw and understood that every Shewing is full of privities [left hid].

And therefore me behoveth now to tell three properties in which I am somewhat eased. The first is the beginning of teaching that I understood therein, in the same time; the second is the inward learning that I have understood therein since; the third, all the whole Revelation from the beginning to the end (that is to say of this Book) which our Lord God of his goodness bringeth oftentimes freely to the sight of mine understanding. And these three are so oned, as to my understanding, that I cannot, nor may, dispart them. And by these three, as one, I have teaching whereby I ought to believe and trust in our Lord God, that of the same goodness of which he shewed it, and for the same end, right so, of the same goodness and for the same end he shall declare it to us when it is his will.

For, twenty years after the time of the Shewing, save three months, I had teaching inwardly, as I shall say. "It belongeth to thee to take heed to all the properties and conditions that were shewed in the example, though thou think that they be misty and indifferent to thy sight." I assented willingly, with great desire, and inwardly [beheld] with avisement all the points and properties that were shewed in the same time, as far forth as my wit and understanding would serve: beginning my beholding at the Lord and at the Servant, and the manner of sitting of the Lord, and the place that he sat on, and the colour of his clothing and the manner of shape, and his countenance[1] without, and his nobleness and his goodness within; at the manner of standing of the Servant, and the place where, and how; at his manner of clothing, the colour and the shape; at his outward having and at his inward goodness and his unlothfulness.

The Lord that sat solemnly in rest and in peace, I under-

[1] MS. "eher" or "ehen", ? "eyes".

stood that he is God. The Servant that stood afore the Lord,
I understood that it was shewed for Adam; that is to say,
one man was shewed, that time, and his falling, to make it
thereby understood how God beholdeth All-Man and his
falling. For in the sight of God all man is one man, and one
man is all man. This man was hurt in his might and made
full feeble; and he was stunned in his understanding, for he
turned from the beholding of his Lord. But his will was kept
whole in God's sight;—for his will I saw our Lord com-
mend and approve. But himself was letted and blinded from
the knowing of this will; and this is to him great sorrow and
grievous dis-ease: for neither doth he see clearly his loving
Lord, which is to him full meek and mild, nor doth he see
truly what himself is in the sight of his loving Lord. And
well I wot when these two are wisely and truly seen, we shall
get rest and peace here in part, and the fulness of the bliss of
Heaven, by his plenteous grace.

And this was a beginning of teaching which I saw in the
same time, whereby I might come to know in what manner
he beholdeth us in our sin. And then I saw that only Pain
blameth and punisheth, and our courteous Lord comforteth
and sorroweth; and ever he is to the soul in glad Cheer,
loving, and longing to bring us to bliss.

The place that the Lord sat on was simple, on the earth,
barren, and desert, alone in wilderness; his clothing was
loose and long[1] and full seemly, as falleth to a Lord; the
colour of his cloth was blue as azure, most sad and fair, his
cheer was merciful; the colour of his face was fair-brown,—
with full seemly features; his eyes were black, most fair and
seemly shewing, full of lovely pity, and within him, an high
regard,[2] long and broad, all full of endless heavens. And the

[1] MS. "wyde and syde", i.e., wide and long.
[2] MS. "within him an *heyward* long and brode, all full of endless hevyns".
Perhaps "hey" has been written as if affixed to "ward", i.e., "regard".

lovely looking wherewith he looked upon his Servant continually,—and especially in his falling,—methought it might
melt our hearts for love and burst them in two for joy. The
fair looking shewed [itself] of a seemly medley which was
marvellous to behold: the one [part] was Ruth and Pity, the
other was Joy and Bliss. The Joy and Bliss passeth as far the
Ruth and Pity as Heaven is above earth: the Pity was earthly
and the Bliss was heavenly: the Ruth and Pity of the Father
was [in regard] of the falling of Adam, which is his most
loved creature; the Joy and Bliss was [in regard] of his dearworthy Son, which is even with the Father. The Merciful
Beholding of his lovely eyes fulfilled all earth and descended
down with Adam into hell, with which continuant pity
Adam was kept from endless death. And thus Mercy and
Pity dwelleth with mankind unto the time we come up into
Heaven.

But man is blinded in this life and therefore we may not
see our Father, God, as he is. And what time that he of his
goodness will shew himself to man, he sheweth himself
homely, as man. Notwithstanding, I saw soothly[1] we ought
to know and believe that the Father is not man.

But his sitting on the earth barren and desert, meaneth
this:—he made man's soul to be his own City and his dwelling-place: which is most pleasing to him of all his works.
And what time that man was fallen into sorrow and pain,
he was not all seemly to serve in that noble office; and therefore our kind Father would prepare[2] himself no other place,
but would sit upon the earth abiding mankind, which is
mingled with earth, till what time by his grace his dearworthy Son had bought again his City into the noble fairness
with his hard travail. The blueness of the clothing betokeneth his steadfastness; the brownness of his fair face, with the
seemly blackness of the eyes, was most according to shew

<hr>

[1] MS. "I reson sothly we owen".      [2] MS. "adyten".

his holy soberness. The largeness of his clothing, which were fair, flaming about, betokeneth that he hath, beclosed in him, all Heavens, and all Joy and Bliss: and this was shewed in a touch [of time], where I say: "Mine understanding was led into the Lord;" in which [inward shewing] I saw him highly joying for the worshipful restoring that he will and shall bring his servant to by his plenteous grace.

And yet I marvelled, beholding the Lord and the Servant aforesaid. I saw the Lord sitting stately, and the Servant standing reverently afore his Lord. In which Servant there is double understanding, one without, another within. Outwardly:—he was clad simply, as a labourer which is disposed for travail, and he stood full near the Lord—not evenly in front[1] of him, but in part to one side, on the left. His clothing was a white kirtle, single, old, and all defaced, dyed with sweat of his body, strait-fitting to him, and short —as it were an handful beneath the knee; [thread]bare, seeming as it should soon be worn out, ready to be ragged and rent. And of this, I marvelled greatly, thinking: this is now an unseemly clothing for the Servant that is so highly loved to stand in afore so worshipful a Lord. And inwardly in him was shewed a ground of love: which love that he had to the Lord was even-like[2] to the love that the Lord had to him.

The wisdom of the Servant saw inwardly that there was one thing to do which should be to the worship of the Lord. And the Servant, for love, having no regard to himself nor to nothing that might befall him, hastily he started and ran at the sending of his Lord, to do that thing which was his will and his worship. For it seemed by his outward clothing as he had been a continuant labourer of long time, and by the inward sight that I had both in the Lord and in the Servant it seemed that he was a new [one], that is to say new

___

[1] MS. "even fornempts", i.e., straight opposite.      [2] i.e., equal.

beginning to travail : which Servant was never sent out afore.

There was a treasure in the earth which the Lord loved. I marvelled and thought what it might be, and I was answered in mine understanding: "It is a meat which is lovesome and pleasant to the Lord." For I saw the Lord sit as a man, and I saw neither meat nor drink wherewith to serve him. This was one marvel. Another marvel was that this solemn Lord had no servant but one, and him he sent out. I beheld, thinking what manner [of] labour it might be that the Servant should do. And then I understood that he should do the greatest labour and hardest travail : that is he should be a gardener, delve and dyke, toil and sweat, and turn the earth upside-down, and seek the deepness, and water the plants in time. And in this he should continue his travail and make sweet floods to run, and noble and plenteous fruits to spring, which he should bring afore the Lord to serve him therewith to his liking. And he should never turn again till he had dressed this meat all ready as he knew that it liked the Lord. And then he should take this meat, with the drink in the meat, and bear it full worshipfully afore the Lord. And all this time the Lord should sit in the same place, abiding his Servant whom he sent out.

And yet I marvelled from whence the Servant came. For I saw in the Lord that he hath within himself endless life, and all manner of goodness, save that treasure that was in the earth. And [also] that [treasure] was grounded in the Lord in marvellous deepness of endless love, but it was not all to his worship till the Servant had thus nobly prepared it,[1] and brought it before him, in himself present. And without the Lord was nothing but wilderness. And I understood not all what this example meant, and therefore I marvelled whence the Servant came.

In the Servant is comprehended the Second Person in the

[1] MS. "dygte".

Trinity; and in the Servant is comprehended Adam: that is to say, All-Man. And therefore when I say the Son, it meaneth the Godhead which is even with the Father; and when I say the Servant, it meaneth Christ's Manhood, which is rightful Adam. By the nearness of the Servant is understood the Son, and by the standing on the left side is understood Adam. The Lord is the Father, God; the Servant is the Son, Christ Jesus; the Holy Ghost is even[1] Love which is in them both.

When Adam fell, God's Son fell: because of the rightful oneing which had been made in heaven, God's Son might not [be disparted] from Adam. (For by Adam I understand All-Man.) Adam fell from life to death, into the deep[2] of this wretched world, and after that into hell: God's Son fell with Adam, into the deep[2] of the Maiden's womb, who was the fairest daughter of Adam; and for this end: to excuse Adam from blame in heaven and in earth; and mightily he fetched him out of hell.

By the wisdom and goodness that was in the Servant is understood God's Son; by the poor clothing as a labourer standing near the left side is understood the Manhood and Adam, with all the mischief and feebleness that followeth. For in all this our good Lord shewed his own Son and Adam but one Man. The virtue and the goodness that we have is of Jesus Christ, the feebleness and the blindness that we have is of Adam: which two were shewed in the Servant.

And thus hath our good Lord Jesus taken upon him all our blame, and therefore our Father nor may nor will more blame assign to us than to his own Son, dearworthy Christ. Thus was he, the Servant, afore his coming into earth standing ready afore the Father in purpose, till what time he would send him to do that worshipful deed by which mankind was brought again into heaven;—that is to say, not-

[1] i.e., equal.          [2] MS, "the slade".

99

withstanding that he is God, even with the Father as anent the Godhead. But in his foreseeing purpose that he would be Man, to save man in fulfilling of his Father's will, so he stood afore his Father as a Servant, willingly[1] taking upon him all our charge. And then he started full readily at the Father's will, and anon he fell full low, into the Maiden's womb, having no regard to himself nor to his hard pains.

The white kirtle is the flesh; the singleness is that there was right naught atwix the Godhead and Manhood; the straitness is poverty; the eld is of Adam's wearing; the defacing of sweat, of Adam's travail; the shortness sheweth the Servant's labour.

And thus I saw the Son saying in his meaning[2]: "Lo, my dear Father, I stand before thee in Adam's kirtle, all ready to start and to run: I would be in the earth to do thy worship when it is thy will to send me. How long shall I desire?" Full soothfastly wist the Son when it would be the Father's will and how long he should desire: that is to say [he wist it] anent the Godhead: for he is the Wisdom of the Father; wherefore this meaning was shewed in understanding of the Manhood of Christ. For all mankind that shall be saved by the sweet Incarnation and blissful Passion of Christ, all is the Manhood of Christ; for he is the Head and we be his members. To which members the day and the time is unknown when every passing woe and sorrow shall have an end, and the everlasting joy and bliss shall be fulfilled; which day and time for to see, all the Company of Heaven longeth. And all that shall be under heaven that shall come thither, their way is by longing and desire. Which desire and longing was shewed in the Servant's standing afore the Lord,—or else thus in the Son's standing afore the Father in Adam's kirtle. For the languor and desire of all Mankind that shall be saved appeared in Jesus: for Jesus is all that shall be saved, and All

---

[1] MS. "wilfully", i.e., of his own will.     [2] i.e., purpose.

that shall be saved is Jesus. And all of the Charity of God; with obedience, meekness, and patience, and virtues that belong to us.

Also in this marvellous example I have teaching with me as it were the beginning of an ABC, whereby I have some understanding of our Lord's meaning. For the privities of the Revelation be hid therein;—notwithstanding that all the Shewings are full of privities. The sitting of the Father betokeneth his Godhead: that is to say, by shewing of rest and peace: for in the Godhead may be no travail. And that he shewed himself as Lord, betokeneth [his governance] to our manhood. The standing of the Servant betokeneth travail; on side, and on the left, betokeneth that he was not all worthy to stand even-right afore the Lord; his starting was the Godhead, and the running was the Manhood: for the Godhead started from the Father into the Maiden's womb, falling into the taking of our kind. And in this falling he took great sore: the sore he took was our flesh, in which he had also swift feeling of deadly pains. By that he stood dreadfully before the Lord and not even-right, betokeneth that his clothing was not honest to stand in even-right afore the Lord, nor that might not, nor should not, be his office while he was a labourer; nor also he might not sit in rest and peace with the Lord till he had won his peace rightfully with his hard travail; and by the left side [betokeneth] that the Father left his own Son, wilfully, in the Manhood to suffer all man's pains, without sparing of him. By that his kirtle was in point to be ragged and rent, is understood the blows[1] and the scourgings, the thorns and the nails, the drawing and the dragging, his tender flesh rending. (As I saw in some part [before] how the flesh was rent from the head-pan, falling in pieces until the time when the bleeding failed, and then it began to dry again, cleaving to the bone.) And by the

[1] MS. "sweppys".

wallowing and writhing, groaning and moaning, is understood that he might never rise almightily from the time that
he was fallen into the Maiden's womb, till his body was
slain and dead, he yielding the soul into the Father's hands
with all Mankind for whom he was sent.

And at this point he began first to shew his might: for
he went into Hell, and when he was there he raised up the
great Root out of the deep deepness which rightfully was
knit to him in high Heaven. The body was in the grave till
Easter-morrow, and from that time he lay nevermore. For
then was rightfully ended the wallowing and the writhing,
the groaning and the moaning. And our foul deadly flesh
that God's Son took on him, which was Adam's old kirtle,
strait, [worn]-bare, and short, then by our Saviour was made
fair, new, white and bright and of endless cleanness; loose
and long;[1] fairer and richer than was then the clothing which
[before] I saw on the Father: for that clothing was blue, but
Christ's clothing is [coloured] now of a fair seemly medley,
which is so marvellous that I can it not describe: for it is all
of very worships.

Now sitteth not the Lord on earth in wilderness, but he
sitteth in his noblest Seat, which he made in Heaven most
to his liking. Now standeth not the Son afore the Father as a
Servant afore the Lord dreadingly, meanly[2] clad, in part
naked; but he standeth afore the Father even-right, richly
clad in blissful largesse, with a Crown upon his head of
precious richness. For it was shewed that we be his Crown:
which Crown is the Father's Joy, the Son's Worship, the
Holy Ghost's liking, and endless marvellous Bliss to all that
be in Heaven. Now standeth not the Son afore the Father on
the left side, as a labourer, but he sitteth on his Father's
right hand, in endless rest and peace. (But it is not meant
that the Son sitteth on the right hand, side by side, as one

[1] MS. "wyde and syde".       [2] MS. "unornely".

man sitteth by another in this life,—for there is no such sitting, as to my sight, in the Trinity,—but he sitteth on his Father's right hand,—that is to say: in the highest nobleness of the Father's joys.) Now is the Spouse, God's Son, in peace with his loved Wife, which is the Fair Maiden of endless Joy. Now sitteth the Son, Very God and Man, in his City in rest and peace: which [City] his Father hath adight to him of his endless purpose; and the Father in the Son; and the Holy Ghost in the Father and in the Son.

## THE FIFTY-SECOND CHAPTER

God rejoiceth that he is our Father, Brother, and Spouse. How the chosen have here a medley of weal and woe; and how we may eschew sin

AND thus I saw that God rejoiceth that he is our Father, and God rejoiceth that he is our Mother, and God rejoiceth that he is our Very Spouse and our soul is his loved Wife. And Christ rejoiceth that he is our Brother, and Jesus rejoiceth that he is our Saviour. These are five high joys, as I understand, in which he willeth that we enjoy; him praising, him thanking, him loving, him endlessly blessing.

All that shall be saved, we have in us, for the time of this life, a marvellous medley both of weal and woe: we have in us our Lord Jesus uprisen, we have in us the wretchedness and the mischief of Adam's falling [and] dying. By Christ we are steadfastly kept, and by his grace touching us we are raised into sure trust of salvation. And by Adam's falling we are so broken, in our feeling, in diverse manners by sins and by sundry pains, in which we are made dark and so blind that scarcely[1] we can take any comfort. But in our

[1] MS. "onethys".

meaning we abide in God, and faithfully trust to have mercy and grace; and this is his own working in us. And of his goodness he openeth the eye of our understanding, by which we have sight, sometime more and sometime less, according as God giveth ability to receive. And now we are raised into the one, and now we are suffered to fall into the other.

And thus is this medley so marvellous in us that scarcely we know of our self or of our even-Christian in what way we stand, for the marvellousness of this sundry feeling. But that same Holy Assent [is] that we assent to God when we feel him, truly willing to be with him, with all our heart, and with all our soul, and with all our might. And then we hate and despise our evil stirrings and all that might be occasion of sin, ghostly and bodily. And yet nevertheless when this sweetness is hid, we fall again into blindness, and so into woe and tribulation in diverse manners. But then is this our comfort, that we know in our faith that by virtue of Christ which is our Keeper, we assent never thereto, but we grudge there-against, and endure, in pain and woe, praying, unto that time that he sheweth him again to us.

And thus we stand in this medley all the days of our life. But he willeth that we trust that he is lastingly with us. And that in three manner. He is with us in Heaven, very Man, in his own Person, us updrawing; and that was shewed in [the Shewing of] the ghostly Thirst. And he is with us in earth, us leading; and that was shewed in the Third [Shewing], where I saw God in a Point. And he is with us in our soul, endlessly dwelling, us ruling and keeping; and that was shewed in the Sixteenth [Shewing], as I shall say.

And thus in the Servant was shewed the scathe and blindness of Adam's falling; and in the Servant was shewed the wisdom and goodness of God's Son. And in the Lord was shewed the ruth and pity of Adam's woe, and in the Lord was shewed the high nobleness and the endless worship that

Mankind is come to by the virtue of the Passion and death of his dearworthy Son. And therefore mightily he joyeth in his falling for the high raising and fulness of bliss that Mankind is come to, overpassing that we should have had if he had not fallen.—And thus to see this overpassing nobleness was mine understanding led into God in the same time that I saw the Servant fall.

And thus we have, now, matter of mourning: for our sin is cause of Christ's pains; and we have, lastingly, matter of joy: for endless love made him to suffer. And therefore the creature that seeth and feeleth the working of love by grace, hateth naught but sin: for of all things, to my sight, love and hate are [the] hardest and most unmeasureable contraries. And notwithstanding all this, I saw and understood in our Lord's meaning that we may not in this life keep us from sin as wholly in full cleanness as we shall be in Heaven. But we may well by grace keep us from the sins which would lead us to endless pains, as Holy Church teacheth us; and eschew venial [sin] reasonably up to our might. And if we by our blindness and our wretchedness any time fall, yet we readily rise, knowing the sweet touching of grace, and wilfully amend us upon the teaching of Holy Church, according as the sin is grievous, and go forthwith to God in love; and neither, on the one side, fall over low, inclining to despair, nor, on the other side, be over-reckless as if we made no matter of it;[1] but nakedly acknowledging our feebleness, [we] wit that we may not stand a twinkling of an eye but by keeping of grace, and reverently cleave to God, on him only trusting.

For after one wise is the Beholding by[2] God, and after another wise is the Beholding by[2] man. For it belongeth to man meekly to accuse himself, and it belongeth to the proper Goodness of our Lord God courteously to excuse

---

[1] MS. "gove no fors", i.e., gave it no force.        [2] MS. "of".

man. And these be two parts that were shewed in the double cheer with which the Lord beheld the falling of his loved Servant. The one was shewed outward, very meekly and mildly, with great ruth and pity; and that of endless Love. And right thus will our Lord that we accuse our self, wilfully and soothly seeing and knowing our falling and all the harms that come thereof; seeing and witting that we can never restore it; and therewith that we wilfully and truly see and know his everlasting love that he hath to us, and his plenteous mercy. And thus graciously to see and know both together is the meek accusing that our Lord asketh of us, and himself worketh it where it is. And this is the lower part of man's life, and it was shewed in the [Lord's] outward cheer. In which shewing I saw two parts: the one is the rueful falling of man, the other is the worshipful Satisfaction[1] that our Lord hath made for man.

The other cheer was shewed inward: and that was more highly and all [fully] one.[2] For the life and the virtue that we have in the lower part is of the higher, and it cometh down to us [from out] of the kind love of the [high] Self, by [the working of] grace. Atwix that one and that other there is right naught: for it is all one love. Which one blessed love hath now, in us, double working: for in the lower part are pains and passions, ruth and pity, mercies and forgiveness, and such other that are profitable; but in the higher part are none of these, but all one high love and marvellous joy: in which marvellous joy all pains are highly restored. And in this [time] our Lord showed not only our excusing[3] from blame, in his beholding of our higher part, but also the worshipful nobleness that he shall bring us to by the working of grace in our lower part, turning all our blame [that is therein, from our falling] into endless worship [when we be oned to the high Self above].

---

[1] MS. "asseth".      [2] MS. "and al on".      [3] i.e., exculpating.

## THE FIFTY-THIRD CHAPTER

The kindness of God assigneth no blame to his chosen,
for in these is a godly will that never consenteth to
sin. For it behoveth the mercy of God to be knit to
these, that there be a substance kept that may never be
parted from him

AND I saw that he willeth that we wit [how] he taketh not
harder the falling of any creature that shall be saved than he
took the falling of Adam, which, we know, was endlessly
loved and securely kept in the time of all his need, and now
is blissfully restored in high overpassing joy. For our Lord
is so good, so gentle, and so courteous, that he may never
assign default in [those by] whom he shall ever be blessed
and praised.

And in this that I have now told was my desire in part
answered, and my great difficulty[1] some deal eased, by the
lovely, gracious Shewing of our good Lord. In which Shewing I saw and understood full surely that in every soul that
shall be saved is a Godly Will that never assented to sin, nor
ever shall: which Will is so good that it may never will evil,
but evermore continually it willeth good, and worketh
good in the sight of God. Therefore our Lord willeth that
we know this in the Faith and the belief; and namely and
truly that we have all this blessed Will whole and safe in our
Lord Jesus Christ. For that same Kind[2] that Heaven shall be
filled with, behoveth needs of God's rightfulness, so to be
knit and oned to him, that therein was kept a substance
which might never, nor should, be parted from him; and
that through his own Good Will in his endless foreseeing
purpose.

But notwithstanding this rightful knitting and this endless

[1] MS. "awer", i.e., awe, perplexity.          [2] i.e., human nature.

107

oneing, yet the redemption and the again-buying of mankind
is needful and speedful in everything, as it is done for the
same intent and to the same end that Holy Church in our
Faith us teacheth.

For I saw that God began never to love mankind: for
right the same that mankind shall be in endless bliss, fulfilling the joy of God as anent his works, right so the same
mankind hath been in the foresight of God, known and loved
from without beginning in his rightful intent. By the endless
assent of the full accord of all the Trinity, the Mid-Person
willed to be Ground and Head of this fair Kind: out of
whom we be all come, in whom we be all enclosed, into
whom we shall all wend,[1] in him finding our full heaven in
everlasting joy, by the foreseeing purpose of all the blessed
Trinity from without beginning.

For ere that he made us he loved us, and when we were
made we loved him. And this is a Love that is made, [by] the
Kindly Substantial Goodness of the Holy Ghost; Mighty, in
reason of the Might of the Father; and Wise in mind of the
Wisdom of the Son. And thus is Man's Soul made by God
and in the same point knit to God.

And thus I understand that man's soul is made of naught:
that is to say, it is made, but of naught that is made. And
thus:—When God should make man's body he took the
slime[2] of earth, which is a matter mingled and gathered of
all bodily things; and thereof he made man's body. But to
the making of man's Soul he would take right naught, but
made it. And thus is the kind made rightfully oned to the
Maker, which is Substantial kind not made; that is, God.
And therefore it is that there may nor shall be right naught
atwix God and man's Soul.

And in this endless Love man's Soul is kept whole, as the
matter of the Revelations meaneth and sheweth: in which

[1] MS. "wynden".        [2] MS. "slyppe".

endless Love we be led and kept of God and never shall be lost. For he willeth we wit that our Soul is a life, which life of his Goodness and his Grace shall last in Heaven without end, him loving, him thanking, him praising. And right the same that we shall be without end, the same we were treasured in God and hid, known and loved from without beginning.

Wherefore he willeth we wit that the noblest thing that ever he made is mankind: and the fullest Substance and the highest Virtue is the blessed Soul of Christ. And furthermore he would have us understand that his dearworthy Soul [of Manhood] was preciously knit to him in the making [by him of Manhood's Substantial Nature] which knot is [so] subtle and so mighty that [it][1] is oned into God: in which oneing it is made endlessly holy. Furthermore he willeth we wit that all the souls that shall be saved in Heaven without end, are knit and oned in this oneing and made holy in this holiness.

## THE FIFTY-FOURTH CHAPTER

We ought to rejoice that God dwelleth in our soul and our soul in God, so that betwixt God and our soul is nothing, but, as it were, all God; and how faith is the ground of all virtue in our soul by the Holy Ghost

AND because of the great, endless love that God hath to all Mankind, he maketh no disparting in love betwixt the blessed Soul of Christ and the least soul that shall be saved. For it is full easy to believe and to trust that the dwelling[2] of the blessed Soul of Christ is full high in the glorious Godhead, and soothly, as I understand in our Lord's meaning,

[1] i.e., the soul of man.          [2] MS. "wonying".

where the blessed Soul of Christ is, there is the Substance of all the souls that shall be saved by Christ.

Highly ought we to rejoice that God dwelleth in our soul, and much more highly ought we to rejoice that our soul dwelleth in God. Our soul is made to be God's dwelling-place; and the dwelling-place of the soul is God, which is unmade. And high understanding it is, inwardly to see and know that God, which is our Maker, dwelleth in our soul; and an higher understanding it is, inwardly to see and to know that our soul, that is made, dwelleth in God's substance: of which substance, God, we are that we are.

And I saw no difference betwixt God and our Substance: but as it were all God; and yet mine understanding took that our Substance is in God: that is to say, that God is God, and our Substance is a creature in God. For the Almighty Truth of the Trinity is our Father: for he made us and keepeth us in him; and the deep Wisdom of the Trinity is our Mother, in whom we are all enclosed; the high Goodness of the Trinity is our Lord, and in him we are enclosed, and he in us. We are enclosed in the Father, and we are enclosed in the Son, and we are enclosed in the Holy Ghost. And the Father is enclosed in us, and the Son is enclosed in us, and the Holy Ghost is enclosed in us: Almightiness, All-Wisdom, All-Goodness: one God, one Lord.

And our faith is a Virtue that cometh of our kind Substance into our Sensual soul by the Holy Ghost; in which all our virtues come to us: for without that, no man may receive virtue. For it is naught else but a right understanding, with true belief, and sure trust, of our Being: that we are in God, and God in us, which we see not. And this virtue, with all other that God hath ordained to us coming therein, worketh in us great things. For Christ's merciful working is in us, and we graciously accord to him through the gifts and the virtues of the Holy Ghost. This working maketh that we are Christ's children, and Christian in living.

## THE FIFTY-FIFTH CHAPTER

Christ is our way, leading and presenting us to the Father, forthwith as the soul is infused into the body, mercy and grace working

AND thus Christ is our Way, us surely leading in his laws, and Christ in his body mightily beareth us up into heaven. For I saw that Christ, us all having in him that shall be saved by him, worshipfully presenteth his Father in heaven with us; which present full thankfully his Father receiveth, and courteously giveth it to his Son, Jesus Christ: which gift and working is joy to the Father, and bliss to the Son, and liking to the Holy Ghost. And of all things that belong to us [to do], it is most liking to our Lord that we joy in this joy which is in the blessed Trinity [in virtue] of our salvation. (And this was seen in the Ninth Shewing, where it speaketh more of this matter.) And notwithstanding all our feeling of woe or weal, God willeth that we should understand and know by faith[1] that we are more verily in heaven than in earth.

Our Faith cometh of the kind Love of our soul, and of the clear light of our Reason, and of the steadfast Mind which we have of God in our first making. And what time that our soul is inspired into our body, in which we are made sensual, all so soon mercy and grace begin to work, having of us care and keeping with pity and love: in which working the Holy Ghost formeth, in our Faith, Hope that we shall

[1] MS. "feythyn".

come again up above to our Substance, into the Virtue of Christ, increased and fulfilled through the Holy Ghost. Thus I understood that the sensuality is grounded in Kind, in Mercy, and in Grace: which Ground [en]ableth us to receive gifts that lead us to endless life.

For I saw full assuredly that our Substance is in God, and also I saw that in our sensuality God is: for in the self[-same] point that our Soul is made sensual, in the self[-same] point is the City of God ordained to him from without beginning; into which See he cometh, and never shall remove [from] it. For God is never out of the soul in which he dwelleth blissfully without end. And this was seen in the Sixteenth Shewing where it saith: "The place that Jesus taketh in our soul: he shall never remove [from] it. And all the gifts that God may give to creatures, he hath given to his Son Jesus for us: which gifts he, dwelling in us, hath enclosed in him unto the time that we be waxen and grown—our soul with our body and our body with our soul, either of them taking help of other—till we be brought up into stature, as kind worketh. And then, in the ground of kind, with working of mercy, the Holy Ghost graciously inspireth into us gifts leading to endless life.

And thus was my understanding led of God to see in him and to understand, to wit and to know, that our soul is made [a] trinity, like to the unmade blissful Trinity,[1] known and loved from without beginning, and in the making oned to the Maker, as it is aforesaid. This sight was full sweet and marvellous to behold, peaceable and restful, sure and delectable.

And because of the worshipful oneing that was thus made by God betwixt the soul and body, it behoveth needs to be that mankind shall be restored from double death: which restoring might never be until the time that the Second

[1] i.e., Wisdom, Truth, Love, or Goodness, *vide supra*, Chap. 44.

Person in the Trinity had taken the lower part of man's kind; to whom the highest [part] was oned in the First-making. And these two parts were in Christ, the higher and the lower: which is but one Soul; the higher part was one in peace with God, in full joy and bliss; the lower part, which is sensuality, suffered for the salvation of mankind.

And these two parts [in Christ] were seen and felt in the Eighth Shewing, in which my body was fulfilled of feeling and mind of Christ's Passion and his death, and furthermore with this was a subtle feeling and privy inward sight of the High Part that I was shewed in the same time when I could not, [even] for the friendly[1] proffer [made to me], look up into Heaven: and that was because of that mighty beholding [that I had] of the Inward Life. Which Inward Life is that High Substance, that precious Soul [of Christ], which is endlessly rejoicing in the Godhead.

## THE FIFTY-SIXTH CHAPTER

It is easier to know God than our own soul, for God is nearer to us than that: therefore, if we will have knowing of it, we must seek into God

AND thus I saw full surely that it is readier to us to come to the knowing of God than to know our own Soul. For our Soul is so deep-grounded in God, and so endlessly treasured, that we may not come to the knowing thereof till we have first knowing of God, which is the Maker, to whom it is oned. But, notwithstanding, I saw that we have, of fulness, to desire wisely and truly to know our own Soul: whereby we are learned to seek it where it is, and that is, in God. And thus by gracious leading of the Holy Ghost, we

---

[1] MS. "wher I myte not for the mene profir lokyn up on to hevyn".

should know them both in one: whether we be stirred to know God or our Soul, both [these stirrings] are good and true.

God is nearer to us than our own Soul: for he is [the] Ground in whom our Soul standeth, and he is [the] Mean that keepeth the Substance and the Sensuality together so that they shall never dispart. For our soul sitteth in God in very rest, and our soul standeth in God in very strength, and our Soul is kindly rooted in God in endless love: and therefore if we will have knowledge of our Soul, and communing and dalliance therewith, it behoveth to seek into our Lord God in whom it is enclosed. And of this enclosing I saw and understood more in the Sixteenth Shewing, as I shall say.

And anent our Substance and our Sensuality [both together] may rightly be called our Soul:[1] and that is because of the oneing that they have in God. The worshipful City that our Lord Jesus sitteth in, it is our Sensuality, in which he is enclosed: and our Kindly Substance is enclosed in Jesus with the blessed Soul of Christ sitting in rest in the Godhead.

And I saw full surely that it behoveth needs to be that we should be in longing and in penance unto the time that we be led so deep into God that we verily and truly know our own Soul. And soothly I saw that into this high deepness our good Lord himself leadeth us in the same love that he made us, and in the same love that he bought us by Mercy and Grace through virtue of his blessed Passion. And notwithstanding all this, we may never come to full knowing of God till we know first clearly our own Soul. For until the time that our Soul is in its full powers[2] we cannot be all full holy:

[1] MS. "& anempts our substance and sensualite it may rytely be clepid our soule".

[2] MS. "the full myts".

and that is [until the time] that our Sensuality by the virtue
of Christ's Passion be brought up to the Substance, with all
the profits of our tribulation that our Lord shall make us
to get by Mercy and Grace.

I had, in part, [experience of the] Touching [of God in
the soul], and it is grounded in kind. That is to say, our
Reason is grounded in God, which is Substantial kindhood.[1]
[Out] of this Substantial kindhood Mercy and Grace springeth and spreadeth into us, working all things in fulfilling of
our joy: these are our Ground in which we have our
Increase and our Fulfilling.

These be three properties in one Goodness: and where
one worketh, all work in the things which be now belong-
ing to us. God willeth that we understand [this], desiring
with all our heart and all our strength to have knowing of
them more and more unto the time that we be fulfilled: for
fully to know them and clearly to see them is naught else
but endless joy and bliss that we shall have in Heaven, which
God willeth should be begun here in knowing of his love.

For by our Reason only we may not profit, but if we have
verily therewith Mind and Love: nor only in our kindly
Ground that we have in God we may not be saved but if we
have, coming of the same Ground, Mercy, and Grace. For
of these three working all together we receive all our Goodness. Of the which the first [gifts] are goods of kind: for in
our First making God gave us as full goods as we might receive only in our spirit—and also greater goods;[2] but his
foreseeing purpose in his endless wisdom willed that we
should be double.

---

[1] MS. "I had in partie touching and it is groundid in kynd: that is to
sey, our reson is groundid in God, which is substantial kyndhede."

[2] MS. "ffor in our first makyng God gaf us as ful goods and also greter
godes as we myte receivin only in our spirite". In the MS. the word
"spirit" is used here only, apparently in the sense of "Substance".

## THE FIFTY-SEVENTH CHAPTER

In our substance we be full, in our sensuality we fail,
which God will repair by mercy and grace. How our
kind which is the higher part is knit to God in the
making, and Jesus is knit to our kind in the lower part,
in our flesh-taking. Mary is our mother

AND anent our Substance he made us noble, and so rich that
evermore we work his will and his worship. (Where I say
"we," it meaneth Man that shall be saved.) For soothly I saw
that we are that which he loveth, and do that which him
liketh, lastingly without any stinting: and [that by virtue] of
the great riches and of the high noble virtues by measure
come to our soul what time it is knit to our body: in which
knitting we are made Sensual.

And thus in our Substance we are full, and in our Sensuality we fail: which failing God will restore and fulfil by
working of Mercy and Grace plenteously flowing into us out
of his own kind Goodness.[1] And thus his kind Goodness
maketh that Mercy and Grace work in us, and the kind
goodness that we have of him enableth us to receive the
working of Mercy and Grace.

I saw that our kind is in God whole: in which [whole
nature of Manhood] he maketh diversities flowing out of
him to work his will: whom kind keepeth, and Mercy and
Grace restoreth and fulfilleth. And of these none shall
perish: for our kind that is the higher part is knit to God in
the making; and God is knit to our kind, that is the lower
part, in our flesh-taking: and thus in Christ our two natures
are oned. For the Trinity is comprehended in Christ, in
whom our higher part is grounded and rooted; and our
lower part the Second Person hath taken: which kind first

[1] MS. "kynde godhede".

116

to him was made ready.[1] For I saw full surely that all the works that God hath done, or ever shall, were fully known to him and aforeseen from without beginning. And for Love he made Mankind and, for the same Love, himself would be Man.

The next Good that we receive is our Faith, in which our profiting beginneth. And it cometh [out] of the high riches of our kind Substance into our Sensual soul, and it is grounded in us and we are in it through the kind Goodness of God, by the working of Mercy and Grace. And thereof come all other goods by which we are led and saved. For the Commandments of God come therein: in which we ought to have two manners of understanding: [the one is that we ought to understand and know] which are his biddings, to love and to keep them; the other is that we ought to know his forbiddings, to hate and to refuse them. For in these two is all our working comprehended. Also in our faith come the Seven Sacraments, each following other in order as God hath ordained them to us: and all manner of virtues.

For the same virtues that we have received of our Substance, given to us in kind by the Goodness of God,—the same virtues by the working of Mercy are given to us in Grace through the Holy Ghost, renewed: which virtues and gifts are treasured to us in Jesus Christ. For in that same[2] time that God knitted him to our body in the Maiden's womb, he took our Sensual soul: in which taking he, us all having enclosed in him, oned it to our Substance: in which oneing he was perfect Man. For Christ having knit in him every[2] man that shall be saved, is perfect Man. Thus our Lady is our Mother in whom we are all enclosed and of her born,[3] in Christ: (for she that is Mother of our Saviour is

---

[1] MS. "adyte".     [2] MS. "ilk".

[3] The MS. has "borne" in both cases, which may mean either *born* or *borne*.

Mother of all that shall be saved in our Saviour;) and our
Saviour is our Very Mother in whom we be endlessly borne,
and never shall come out of him.

Plenteously and fully and sweetly was this shewed, and
it is spoken of in the First [Shewing], where it saith: "We
are all in him enclosed and he is enclosed in us." And that
[enclosing of him in us] is spoken of in the Sixteenth Shewing, where it saith "He sitteth in our soul."

For it is his liking to reign in our Understanding blissfully, and sit in our Soul restfully, and to dwell in our Soul
endlessly, us all working into him: in which working he
willeth that we be his helpers, giving to him all our attending, learning his lore, keeping his laws, desiring that all be
done that he doeth; truly trusting in him.

For soothly I saw that our Substance is in God.[1]

## THE FIFTY-EIGHTH CHAPTER

God was never displeased with his chosen wife. Of
three properties in the Trinity: Fatherhood, Motherhood, and Lordhood. How our substance is in every
person, but our sensuality is in Christ alone

GOD, the blessed Trinity, which is everlasting Being, right
as he is endless from without beginning, right so it was in
his purpose endless, to make Mankind. Which fair Kind
first was made ready for[2] his own Son, the Second Person.
And when he would, by full accord of all the Trinity, he
made us all at once; and in our making he knit us and oned
us to himself: by which oneing we are kept as clear and as
noble as we were made. By the virtue of the same precious
oneing, we love our Maker and like him, praise him and

[1] See Note 5, *infra*, p. 175.     [2] MS. "adyte to".

thank him, and endlessly joy in him. And this is the work which is wrought continually in every soul that shall be saved: which is the Godly Will aforesaid. And thus in our making, God, Almighty, is our kindly Father; and God, All-Wisdom, is our kindly Mother; with the Love and the Goodness of the Holy Ghost: which is all one God, one Lord. And in the knitting and in the oneing he is our Very, True Spouse, and we his loved Wife and his Fair Maiden: with which Wife he is never displeased. For he saith: I love thee and thou lovest me, and our love shall never be disparted in two.

I beheld the working of all the blessed Trinity, in which beholding I saw and understood these three properties: the property of the Fatherhood, the property of the Mother-hood, and the property of the Lordhood, in one God. In our Father Almighty we have our keeping and our bliss as anent our kindly Substance, which is to us by our making, without beginning. And in the Second Person in wit and wisdom we have our keeping as anent our Sensuality: our restoring and our saving; for he is our Mother, Brother, and Saviour. And in our good Lord, the Holy Ghost, we have our rewarding and our resting for our living and our travail, and endless overpassing of all that we desire, in his marvellous courtesy, of his high plenteous grace.

For all our life is in three: in the first we have our Being, in the second we have our Increasing, and in the third we have our Fulfilling: the first is Kind, the second is Mercy, and the third is Grace.

For the first, I saw and understood that the high Might of the Trinity is our Father, and the deep Wisdom of the Trinity is our Mother, and the great Love of the Trinity is our Lord: and all this have we in kind and in making of our Substance.[1]

[1] MS. "In our substantiall makyng".

And furthermore I saw that the Second Person, which is our Mother as anent the Substance,[1] that same dearworthy Person is become our Mother as anent the Sense-soul.[2] For we are doubly by God's making: that is to say, Substantial and Sensual. Our Substance is the higher part, which we have in our Father, God Almighty; and the Second Person of the Trinity is our Mother in kind, in making of our Substance,[3] in whom we are grounded and rooted. And he is our Mother in Mercy, in our Sensuality taking. And thus our Mother is to us in diverse manners working: in whom our parts are kept undisparted. For in our Mother Christ we profit and increase, and in Mercy he reformeth us and restoreth, and, by the virtue of his Passion and his Death and Uprising, oneth us to our Substance. Thus worketh our Mother in Mercy to all his children which are to him buxom and obedient.

And Grace worketh with Mercy, and specially in two properties, as it was shewed: which working belongeth to the Third Person, the Holy Ghost. He worketh rewarding and giving. Rewarding is a large giving-of-truth that the Lord doeth to him that hath travailed; and giving is a courteous working which he doeth freely of Grace, fulfilling and overpassing all that is deserved of creatures.

Thus in our Father, God Almighty, we have our being and in our Mother of Mercy we have our reforming and restoring: in whom our Parts are oned and all made perfect Man; and by [reward-]yielding and giving in Grace of the Holy Ghost, we are fulfilled.

And our Substance is [in] our Father, God Almighty, and our Substance is [in] our Mother, God, All-wisdom; and our Substance is in our Lord the Holy Ghost, God All-Goodness. For our Substance is whole in each Person of the

---

[1] MS. "our Mother substantial".          [2] MS. "our Mother sensual".

[3] MS. "our substantiall makyng".

Trinity, which is one God. And our Sensuality is only in the Second Person Christ Jesus: in whom is the Father and the Holy Ghost: and in him and by him we are mightily taken out of Hell, and out of the wretchedness in Earth worshipfully brought up into Heaven and blissfully oned to our Substance: increased in riches and in nobleness by all the virtues of Christ, and by the grace and working of the Holy Ghost.

## THE FIFTY-NINTH CHAPTER

Wickedness is turned into bliss by mercy and grace in the chosen, for the property of God is to do good against ill, by Jesus our Mother in kind grace

AND all this bliss we have by Mercy and Grace: which manner of bliss we might never have had nor known but if that property of Goodness which is God had been contraried: whereby we have this bliss. For wickedness hath been suffered to rise contrary to the Goodness, and the Goodness of Mercy and Grace contraried against the wickedness and turned all to goodness and to worship, to all these that shall be saved. For it is the property in God which doeth good against evil. Thus Jesus Christ that doeth good against evil is our Very Mother: we have our Being of him— where the Ground of Motherhood beginneth—with all the sweet Keeping of Love that endlessly followeth. As verily as God is our Father, so verily God is our Mother; and that shewed he in all, and especially in these sweet words where he saith: "I it am." That is to say, "I it am, the Might and the Goodness of the Fatherhood; I it am, the Wisdom of the Motherhood; I it am, the Light and the Grace that is all blessed Love: I it am, the Trinity, I it am, the Unity: I am the sovereign Goodness of all manner of things. I am that maketh thee to love: I am that maketh thee to long: I it am, the endless fulfilling of all true desires."

For there the soul is highest, noblest, and worthiest, where it is lowest, meekest, and mildest: and [out] of this Substantial Ground we have all our virtues in our Sensuality by gift of kind, by helping and speeding of Mercy and Grace: without the which we may not profit.

Our high Father, God Almighty, which is Being, he knew and loved us from afore any time: of which knowing, in his marvellous deep charity and the foreseeing counsel of all the blessed Trinity, he willed that the Second Person should become our Mother, our Brother, and our Saviour. Wherefore it followeth that, as verily as God is our Father, so verily God is our Mother. Our Father [willeth], our Mother worketh, our good Lord the Holy Ghost confirmeth: and therefore it belongeth to us to love our God in whom we have our being: him reverently thanking and praising for[1] our making, mightily praying to our Mother for[1] mercy and pity, and to our Lord the Holy Ghost for[1] help and grace.

For in these three is all our life: Kind, Mercy, Grace: whereof we have meekness, mildness, patience, and pity; and hating of sin and wickedness—for it belongeth properly to virtue to hate sin and wickedness. And thus is Jesus our Very Mother in kind [by virtue] of our first making; and he is our Very Mother in Grace, by taking our kind made. All the fair working, and all the sweet natural office of dearworthy Motherhood is appropriate[2] to the Second Person: for in him we have this Godly Will whole and safe without end, both in kind and in Grace, of his own proper Goodness. I understood three manners of beholding of Motherhood in God: the first is grounded in our kind making; the second is taking of our kind—and there beginneth the Motherhood

[1] MS. "of".      [2] MS. "impropried".

of Grace; the third is Motherhood of working—and therein
is a forth-spreading by the same Grace, of length and
breadth and of height and of deepness without end. And all
is one Love.

## THE SIXTIETH CHAPTER

Of our sweet, kind, ever-loving Mother, Jesus: and of
the property of motherhood. Jesus is our very Mother,
not feeding us with milk, but with himself; opening his
side to us, and challenging all our love

BUT now behoveth to say a little more of this forth-spreading, as I understand in the meaning of our Lord: how that
we be brought again by the Motherhood of Mercy and
Grace into our Nature's place,[1] where that we were made
by the Motherhood of kind Love: which Kindly-love, it
never leaveth us.

Our Kind Mother, our Gracious Mother,[2] for that he
would all wholly become our Mother in all things, he took
the ground of his Works full low and full mildly in the
Maiden's womb. (And that he shewed in the First [Shewing]
where he brought that meek Maid afore the eye of mine
understanding in the simple stature as she was when she
conceived.) That is to say: our high God is sovereign Wisdom of all: in this low place he arrayed and dight him full
ready in our poor flesh, himself to do the service and the
office of Motherhood in all things.

The Mother's service is nearest, readiest, and surest:
[nearest, for it is most of nature; readiest, for it is most of
love; and surest[3]] for it is most of truth. This office none

[1] MS. "kyndly-stede".
[2] i.e., our Mother by Nature, our Mother in Grace.
[3] These clauses, omitted from the MS., are in Cressy's version.

might, nor could, nor ever should do to the full, but he alone. We wit that all our mother's bearing is [bearing of] us to pain and to dying: and what is this but that our Very Mother, Jesus, he—All-Love—beareth us to joy and to endless living?—blessed may he be! Thus he sustaineth us within himself in love; and travailed, unto the full time that he would suffer the sharpest throes and the grievousest pains that ever were or ever shall be; and died at the last. And when he had [so] done, and so borne us to bliss, yet might not all this make full content[1] to his marvellous love; and that sheweth he in these high overpassing words of love: "If I might suffer more, I would suffer more."

He might no more die, but he would not stint of working: wherefore then it behoveth him to feed us; for the dearworthy love of Motherhood hath made him debtor to us. The mother may give her child suck [of] her milk, but our precious Mother, Jesus, he may feed us with himself, and doeth it, full courteously and full tenderly, with the Blessed Sacrament that is precious food of very life; and with all the sweet Sacraments he sustaineth us full mercifully and graciously. And so meant he in this blessed word where that he said: "I it am that Holy Church preacheth thee and teacheth thee." That is to say: "All the health and life of Sacraments, all the virtue and grace of my Word, all the Goodness that is ordained in Holy Church for thee, I it am." The mother may lay the child tenderly to her breast, but our tender Mother, Jesus, he may homely lead us into his blessed breast, by his sweet open side, and shew therein part of the Godhead and the joys of Heaven, with ghostly sureness of endless bliss. And that shewed he in the Tenth [Shewing], giving the same understanding in this sweet word where he saith: "Lo! how I loved thee;" beholding into his side, rejoicing.

[1] MS. "makyn asseth".

This fair lovely word *Mother*, it is so sweet and so kind itself[1] that it may not verily be said of none but of him; and to her that is very Mother of him and of all. To the property of Motherhood belongeth kind love, wisdom, and knowing; and it is good: for though it be so that our bodily forthbringing be but little, low, and simple in regard of our ghostly forthbringing, yet it is he that doeth it in the creatures by whom that it is done. The kind, loving Mother that witteth and knoweth the need of her child, she keepeth it full tenderly, as the kind and condition of Motherhood will. And as it waxeth in age, she changeth her working, but not her love. And when it is waxen of more age, she suffereth that it be beaten[2] in breaking down of vices, to make the child receive virtues and graces. This working, with all that be fair and good, our Lord doeth it in them by whom it is done: thus he is our Mother in kind by the working of Grace in the lower part for love of the higher part. And he willeth that we know this: for he will have all our love fastened to him. And in this I saw that all our duty that we owe, by God's bidding, to Fatherhood and Motherhood, for [reason of] God's Fatherhood and Motherhood is fulfilled in true loving of God; which blessed love Christ worketh in us. And this was shewed in all [the Revelations] and especially in the high plenteous words where he saith: "It is I that thou lovest."

[1] MS. "so kynd of the self".          [2] MS. "bristinid".

## THE SIXTY-FIRST CHAPTER

*Jesus suffereth us to fall and happily raiseth us; not breaking his love for our trespass, for he willeth that we have the property of a child, fleeing to him alway in our necessity*

AND in our ghostly forthbringing he useth more tenderness of keeping, without any likeness: by as much as our soul is of more price in his sight. He kindleth our understanding, he directeth our ways, he easeth our conscience, he comforteth our soul, he lighteneth our heart, and giveth us, in part, knowing and believing in his blissful Godhead, with gracious mind in his sweet Manhood and his blessed Passion, with courteous marvelling in his high, overpassing Goodness; and maketh us to love all that he loveth, for his love, and to be well paid with him and all his works. And when we fall, hastily he raiseth us by his lovely clasping[1] and gracious touching. And when we be thus strengthened by his sweet working, then we wilfully choose him, by his sweet grace, to be his servants and his lovers lastingly without end.

And after this he suffereth some of us to fall more hard and more grievously than ever we did afore, as us thinketh. And then ween we (who be not all wise) that all were naught that we have begun. But it is not so. For it needeth us to fall, and it needeth us to see it. For if we never fell, we should not know how feeble and how wretched we are of our self, and also we should not fully know that marvellous love of our Maker. For we shall see verily in heaven, without end, that we have grievously sinned in this life, and notwithstanding this, we shall see that we were never hurt in his love, nor were never the less of price in his sight. And by the assay of this falling we shall have an high, marvellous

[1] MS. "clepyng".

knowing of love in God, without end. For hard and marvellous is that love which may not, nor will not, be broken for trespass. And this is one understanding of profit. Another is the lowness and meekness that we shall get by the sight of our falling: for thereby we shall highly be raised in heaven; to which raising we might[1] never have come without that meekness. And therefore it needeth us to see it; and if we see it not, though we fell it should not profit us. And commonly, first we fall and later[2] we see it: and both of the Mercy of God.

The mother may suffer the child to fall sometimes, and be dis-eased in diverse manners for its own profit, but she may never suffer that any manner of peril come to the child, for love. And though our earthly mother may suffer her child to perish, our heavenly Mother, Jesus, may not suffer us that are his children to perish: for he is All-Mighty, All-wisdom, and All-love; and so is none but he—blessed may he be!

But oftentimes when our falling and our wretchedness is shewed us, we are so sore adread, and so greatly ashamed of our self, that scarcely we wit where we may hold us. But then willeth not our courteous Mother that we flee away, for him were nothing lother. But he willeth then that we use the condition of a child: for when it is dis-eased, or adread, it runneth hastily to the mother for help, with all its might. So willeth he that we do, as a meek child saying thus: "My kind Mother, my Gracious Mother, my dearworthy Mother, have mercy on me: I have made myself foul and unlike to thee, and I nor may nor can amend it but with thy privy help and grace." And if we feel us not then eased forthwith, be we sure that he useth the condition of a wise mother. For if he see that it be more profit to us to mourn and to weep, he suffereth it, with ruth and pity, unto the

[1] i.e., could.  [2] MS. "syth".

best time, for love. And he willeth then that we use the property of a child, that evermore kindly trusteth to the love of the mother in weal and in woe.

And he willeth that we take us mightily to the Faith of Holy Church and find there our dearworthy Mother, in solace of true Understanding, with all the communion of the blessed.[1] For one single person may oftentimes be broken, as it seemeth to himself, but the whole Body of Holy Church was never broken, nor never shall be, without end. And therefore a sure thing it is, a good and a gracious, to will meekly and mightily to be fastened and oned to our Mother, Holy Church, that is, Christ Jesus. For the food of mercy that is his dearworthy blood and precious water is plenteous to make us fair and clean; the blessed wounds of our Saviour be open and enjoy to heal us; the sweet, gracious hands of our Mother be ready and diligently about us. For he in all this working useth the office of a kind nurse that hath naught else to do but to give heed about[2] the salvation of her child.

It is his office to save us: it is his worship to do [for] us,[3] and it is his will [that] we know it: for he willeth that we love him sweetly and trust in him meekly and mightily. And this shewed he in these gracious words: "I keep thee full surely."

[1] MS. "all the blessed comon".     [2] MS. "entendyn about".

[3] The MS. seems to have: "to don us", possibly for "to work at us", to perfect our salvation.

## THE SIXTY-SECOND CHAPTER

The Love of God never suffereth his chosen to lose time,
for all their trouble is turned into endless joy

FOR in that time he shewed our frailty and our fallings, our
afflictings and our settings at naught,[1] our despites and our
outcastings, and all our woe so far forth as methought it
might befall in this life. And therewith he shewed his
blessed Might, his blessed Wisdom, his blessed Love: that
he keepeth us in this time as tenderly and as sweetly to his
worship, and as surely to our salvation, as he doeth when we
are in most solace and comfort. And thereto he raiseth us
ghostly and highly in heaven, and turneth it all to his worship and to our joy, without end. For his love suffereth us
never to lose time.

And all this is of the kind-Goodness of God, by the working of Grace. God is kind in his being: that is to say, that
Goodness that is kind, it is God. He is the ground, he is the
substance, he is the same thing that is kind-head. And he is
very Father and very Mother of kind: and all kinds that he
hath made to flow out of him to work his will shall be restored and brought again into him by the salvation of man
through the working of grace.

For of all kinds that he hath set in diverse creatures by
part, in man is all the whole; in fulness and in virtue, in fairness and in goodness, in royalty and nobleness, in all manner
of solemnity, of preciousness and worship. Here may we
see that we are all beholden to God for [our] kind, and we
are all beholden to God for grace. Here may we see us
needeth not greatly to seek far out to know sundry kinds,
but to Holy Church, into our Mother's breast: that is to
say, into our own soul where our Lord dwelleth; and there

---

[1] MS. "our brekyngs and our nowtyngs".

shall we find all now in faith and in understanding. And afterward verily in himself clearly, in bliss.

But [let] no man nor woman take this singularly to himself: for it is not so, it is general: for it is [of] our precious Christ, and to him was this fair nature adight[1] for the worship and nobility of man's making, and for the joy and the bliss of man's salvation; even as he saw, wist, and knew from without beginning.

## THE SIXTY-THIRD CHAPTER

### Sin is more painful than hell, and vile and hurting to kind, but grace saveth kind and destroyeth sin

HERE may we see that we have verily of Kind to hate sin, and we have verily of Grace to hate sin. For Kind is all good and fair in itself, and Grace was sent out to save kind and destroy sin, and bring again fair kind to the blessed point from whence it came: that is God; with more nobleness and worship by the virtuous working of grace. For it shall be seen afore God by all his Holy in joy without end that kind hath been assayed in the fire of tribulation and therein hath been found no flaw, no fault.[2] Thus are Kind and Grace of one accord: for Grace is [of] God, as Kind is [of] God: he is two in manner of working and one in love; and neither of these worketh without other: nor [may they] be disparted.

And when we by Mercy of God and with his help accord us to Kind and Grace, we shall see verily that sin is in sooth viler and painfuller than hell, without likeness: for it is contrary to our fair kind. For as soothly as sin is unclean, so soothly is it unkind, and thus an horrible thing to see for the

[1] i.e., made ready.    [2] MS. "no lak, no defaute".

loved soul that would be all fair and OF DIVINE LOVE
God, as Kind and Grace teacheth.          in the sight of
Yet be we not adread of this, save ina.
speed us : but meekly make we our moan t..s dread may
Mother, and he shall besprinkle us in his precearworthy
make our soul full soft and full mild, and heal blood and
process of time, right as it is most worship to him fair by
to us without end. And of this sweet fair working d joy
never cease nor stint till all his dearworthy children be b all
and forth-brought. (And that shewed he where he shewe
understanding of the ghostly Thirst, that is the love-longing
that shall last until Doomsday.)

Thus in [our] Very Mother, Jesus, our life is grounded,
in the foreseeing Wisdom of himself from without beginning, with the high Might of the Father, the high sovereign
Goodness of the Holy Ghost. And in the taking of our kind
he quickened us ; in his blessed dying upon the Cross he bare
us to endless life ; and from that time, and now, and evermore unto Doomsday, he feedeth us and furthereth us : right
as that high sovereign Kindness of Motherhood, and as
kindly need of Childhood asketh.

Fair and sweet is our Heavenly Mother in the sight of our
souls ; precious and lovely are the Gracious Children in the
sight of our Heavenly Mother, with mildness and meekness,
and all the fair virtues that belong to children in kind. For
kindly the Child despaireth not of the Mother's love, kindly
the Child presumeth not of itself, kindly the Child loveth
the Mother and each one of the other [children]. These are
the fair virtues, with all other that be like, wherewith our
Heavenly Mother is served and pleased.

And I understood none higher stature in this life than
Childhood, in feebleness and failing of might and of wit,
unto the time that our Gracious Mother hath brought us up
to our Father's Bliss. And then shall verily be made known

REVELATION those sweet words where he saith: "All
to us his me... thou shalt see, thyself, that all manner
shall be well." And then shall the Bliss of our Mother,
thing sha...new to begin in the Joys of our God: which
in Chris...ng shall last without end, new beginning.
new b...understood that all his blessed children which be
That...ut of him by Kind shall be brought again into him by
con...
G...e.

## THE SIXTY-FOURTH CHAPTER

The Fifteenth Revelation is as it is shewed. How the
absence of God in this life is our full great pain, beside
other travail

AFORE this time I had great longing and desire of God's
gift to be delivered of this world and of this life. For oftentimes I beheld the woe that is here, and the weal and the
bliss that is being there: (and if there had been no pain in this
life but the absence of our Lord, methought it was sometime more than I might bear;) and this made me to mourn,
and eagerly to long. And also from mine own wretchedness,
sloth, and weakness, me liked not to live and to travail, as
me fell to do.

And to all this our courteous Lord answered for comfort and patience, and said these words: "Suddenly thou
shalt be taken from all thy pain, from all thy sickness, from
all thy dis-ease, and from all thy woe. And thou shalt come
up above and thou shalt have me to thy meed, and thou
shalt be fulfilled of love and of bliss. And thou shalt never
have no manner of pain, no manner of misliking, no wanting
of will; but ever joy and bliss without end. What should it
then aggrieve thee to suffer awhile, seeing that it is my will
and my worship?"

And in this word: "Suddenly thou shalt be taken"—I saw that God rewardeth man for the patience that he hath in abiding God's will, and for his time, and [for] that man lengtheneth his patience over the time of his living. For not-knowing of his time of passing, that is a great profit: for if a man knew his time, he should not have patience over that time; but, as God willeth, while the soul is in the body it seemeth to itself that it is ever at the point to be taken. For all this life and this languor that we have here is but a point, and when we are taken suddenly out of pain into bliss then pain shall be naught.

And in this time I saw a body lying on the earth, which body shewed heavy and ugly, without shape and form, as it were a swollen quag of stinking mire.[1] And suddenly out of this body sprang a full fair creature, a little Child, fully shapen and formed, nimble[2] and lively, whiter than lily: which swiftly[3] glided up into heaven. And the swollenness of the body betokeneth great wretchedness of our deadly flesh, and the littleness of the Child betokeneth the cleanness of purity in the soul. And methought: "With this body abideth[4] no fairness of this Child, and on this Child dwelleth no foulness of this body."

It is full blissful that man be taken from pain, more than that pain be taken from man; for if pain be taken from us it may come again: therefore it is a sovereign comfort and blissful beholding in a loving soul that we shall be taken from pain. For in this behest[5] I saw a marvellous compassion that our Lord hath for us in our woe, and a courteous promising[6] of clear deliverance. For he willeth that we be comforted in the overpassing; and that he shewed in these words: "And thou shalt come up above, and thou shalt have me

---

[1] MS. "a bolned quave of styngand myre".
[2] MS. "swifie", i.e., agile.    [3] MS. "sharply".    [4] MS. "beleveth".
[5] i.e., promise.    [6] MS. "behoting".

to thy meed, and thou shalt be fulfilled of joy and of bliss."

It is God's will that we set the point of our thought in this blissful beholding as often as we may—and as long time keep us therein with his grace; for this is a blessed contemplation to the soul that is led of God, and full greatly to his worship, for the time that it lasteth. And [when] we fall again to our heaviness, and ghostly blindness, and feeling of pains ghostly and bodily, by our frailty, it is God's will that we know that he hath not forgotten us. And so meaneth he in these words, and saith for comfort: "And thou shalt never more have pain; no manner of sickness, no manner of misliking, no wanting of will; but ever joy and bliss without end. What should it then aggrieve thee to suffer awhile, seeing it is my will and my worship?"

It is God's will that we take his behests and his comfortings as largely and as mightily as we may take them, and also he willeth that we take our abiding and our dis-eases as lightly as we may take them, and set them at naught. For the more lightly we take them, and the less price we set on them, for love, the less pain we shall have in the feeling of them, and the more thanks and meed shall we have for them.

## THE SIXTY-FIFTH CHAPTER

How he that chooseth God for love, with reverend meekness, is sure to be saved: which reverend meekness seeth the Lord marvellous great and the self marvellous little; and it is God's will we dread nothing but him

AND thus I understood that what man or woman wilfully chooseth God in this life, for love, he may be sure that he is loved without end: which endless love worketh in him that grace. For he willeth that we keep this trustily, and that we be all secure in hope of the bliss of heaven while we are here, as we shall be in sureness when we are there. And ever the more liking and joy that we take in this sureness, with reverence and meekness, the better it liketh him, as it was shewed. This reverence that I mean is a holy courteous dread of our Lord, to which meekness is knit: and that is, that a creature seeth the Lord marvellous great, and itself marvellous little. For these virtues are had endlessly by the loved of God, and this may now be seen and felt in measure by the gracious presence of our Lord when it is [felt]: which presence in all things is most desired, for it worketh marvellous sureness in true faith, and sure hope, by greatness of charity, in dread that is sweet and delectable.

It is God's will that I see myself as much beholden to him in love as if he had done for me [alone] all that he hath done; and thus should every soul think inwardly of its Lover. That is to say, the Charity of God maketh in us such a unity that, when it is truly seen, no man can part himself from other. And thus ought our soul to think that God hath done for it [alone] all that he hath done.

And this sheweth he to make us to love him and naught dread but him. For it is his will that we wit that all the might of our Enemy is taken into our Friend's hand; and therefore the soul that wotteth assuredly this, it shall not dread [any] but him that it loveth. All other dread it setteth among passions and bodily sickness and imaginations. And therefore though we be in so much pain, woe, and dis-ease that it seemeth to us we can think [of] right naught but [of] that [pain] we are in, or that [which] we feel, [yet] as soon as we may, pass we lightly over, and set we it at naught. And why? For that God killeth we know [him]; and if we know him and love him and reverently dread him, we shall have peace, and be in great rest, and it shall be great liking to us, all that he doeth. And this shewed our Lord in these words: "What should it then aggrieve thee to suffer awhile, seeing it is my will and my worship?"

Now have I told you of Fifteen Revelations, as God vouchsafed to minister them to [my] mind, renewed by lightings and touchings, I hope of the same Spirit that shewed them all.

Of which Fifteen Shewings the First began early in the morn, about the hour of four; and they lasted, shewing by process full fair and steadily, each following other, till it was nine of the day, overpassed.

## THE SIXTY-SIXTH CHAPTER

The Sixteenth Revelation is a conclusion and confirmation to all Fifteen. Of her frailty and mourning in disease, and light speaking after the great comfort of Jesus:
yet the devil, after that, had great power to vex her

AND after this the good Lord shewed the Sixteenth [Revelation] on the night following, as I shall say after: which Sixteenth was conclusion and confirmation to all Fifteen.

But first me behoveth to tell you as anent my feebleness, wretchedness, and blindness—I have said in the beginning: "And in this [moment] all my pain was suddenly taken from me:" of which pain I had no grief nor dis-ease as long as the Fifteen Shewings lasted following. And at the end all was close, and I saw no more. And soon I felt that I should live and languish;[1] and anon my sickness came again: first in my head with a sound and a din, and suddenly all my body was fulfilled with sickness like as it was afore. And I was as barren and as dry as [if] I never had comfort but little. And

[1] MS. "langiren".

136

as a wretch I moaned and cried for feeling of my bodily pains and for failing of comfort, ghostly and bodily.

Then came a Religious person to me and asked me how I fared. I said I had raved to-day. And he laughed loud and inwardly. And I said: "The Cross that stood afore my face, methought it bled fast." And with this word the person that I spake to waxed all sad and marvelled. And anon I was sore ashamed and astonished for my recklessness, and I thought: "This man taketh sadly[1] the least word that I might say." Then said I no more thereof. And when I saw that he took it sadly and with so great reverence, I wept, full greatly ashamed, and would have been shriven; but at that time I could tell it no priest, for I thought: "How should a priest believe me? I believe not our Lord God." This [Shewing] I believed soothfastly for the time that I saw him, and so was then my will and my meaning ever for to do without end; but as a fool I let it pass from my mind. Ah! lo, wretch that I am! this was a great sin, great unkindness, that I for folly of feeling of a little bodily pain, so unwisely lost for the time the comfort of all this blessed Shewing of our Lord God. Here may you see what I am of myself.

But herein would our Courteous Lord not leave me. And I lay still till night, trusting in his mercy, and then I began to sleep. And in the sleep, at the beginning, methought the Fiend set him on my throat, putting forth a visage full near my face, like a young man's, and it was long and wondrous lean: I saw never none such. The colour was red like the tilestone when it is new-burnt, with black spots therein like black freckles—fouler than the tilestone. His hair was red as rust, clipped afore,[2] with full locks hanging on the temples. He grinned on me with a malicious semblance,[3] shew-

---

[1] i.e., solemnly, in earnest.
[2] MS. "evisid aforn with syde lokks hongyng on the thounys".
[3] MS. "shrewd semelant".

ing white teeth: and so much methought it the more horrible. Body nor hands had he none shapely, but with his paws he held me in the throat, and would have strangled me, but he might not.

This ugly Shewing was made [whilst I was] sleeping, and so was none other. But in all this time I trusted to be saved and kept by the mercy of God. And our Courteous Lord gave me grace to waken; and scarcely had I my life. The persons that were with me beheld me, and wet my temples, and my heart began to comfort. And anon a light smoke came in the door, with a great heat and a foul stench.[1] I said: "Benedicite Domine! it is all on fire that is here!" And I weened it had been a bodily fire that should have burnt us all to death. I asked them that were with me if they felt any stench. They said, Nay: they felt none. I said: "Blessed be God!" For that I wist well it was the Fiend that was come to tempest me. And anon I took to that [which] our Lord had shewed me on the same day, with all the Faith of Holy Church (for I beheld it is both one) and fled thereto as to my comfort. And anon all vanished away, and I was brought to great rest and peace, without sickness of body or dread of conscience.

## THE SIXTY-SEVENTH CHAPTER

Of the worshipfulness of the soul, which is so nobly made that it might not better be made; in which the Trinity rejoiceth everlastingly. The soul may have rest in nothing but God, which sitteth therein ruling all things

AND then our Lord opened my ghostly eye and shewed me my soul in midst of my heart. I saw the Soul so large as it

[1] MS. "stinke".

were an endless world, and as it were a blissful kingdom. And by the conditions that I saw therein I understood that it is a worshipful City. In the midst of that City sitteth our Lord Jesus, God and Man, a fair Person of large stature, highest Bishop, solemnest King, most worshipful Lord; and I saw him clad solemnly. And worshipfully he sitteth in the Soul, even-right in peace and rest. And the God-head ruleth and sustaineth[1] heaven and earth and all that is— sovereign Might, sovereign Wisdom, and sovereign Good-ness—[and] the place that Jesus taketh in our Soul he shall never remove it, without end, as to my sight: for in us is his homeliest home and his endless dwelling.[2]

And in this [sight] he shewed the satisfying that he hath of the making of Man's Soul. For as well as the Father might make a creature, and as well as the Son could make a crea-ture, so well would the Holy Ghost that Man's Soul were made: and so it was done. And therefore the blessed Trinity enjoyeth without end in the making of Man's Soul: for he saw from without beginning what should liken him without end. All thing that he hath made sheweth his Lordship— as understanding was given at the same time by example of a creature that is to see great treasures[3] and kingdoms belong-ing to a lord; and when it had seen all the nobleness beneath, then, marvelling, it was stirred to seek above to the high place where the lord dwelleth, knowing, by reason, that his dwelling is in the worthiest place. And thus I understood soothly that our Soul may never have rest in things that are beneath itself. And when it cometh above all creatures into the Self, yet may it not abide in the beholding of its Self, but all the beholding is blissfully set in God that is the Maker dwelling therein. For in Man's Soul is his very dwelling; and the highest light and the brightest shining of the City is the glorious love of our Lord, as to my sight.

And what may make us more to enjoy in God than to see

[1] MS. "gemeth".     [2] MS. "woning".     [3] MS. "noblyes".

in him that he enjoyeth in the highest of all his works? For I saw in the same Shewing that if the blessed Trinity might have made Man's Soul any better, any fairer, any nobler than it was made, he should not have been full pleased with the making of Man's Soul. And he willeth that our hearts be mightily raised above the deepness of the earth and all vain sorrows, and rejoice[1] in him.

## THE SIXTY-EIGHTH CHAPTER

Of soothfast knowing that it is Jesus that showed all this and it was no raving; and how we ought to have sure trust in all our tribulations that we shall not be overcome

THIS was a delectable Sight and a restful Shewing, that it is so without end. The beholding of this while we are here is full pleasant to God and full great speed to us; and the soul that thus beholdeth, it maketh it like to him that is beheld, and oneth it in rest and peace by his grace. And this was a singular joy and bliss to me that I saw him sitting: for the secureness of sitting sheweth endless dwelling.

And he gave me to know soothfastly that it was he that shewed me all afore. And when I had beheld this with avisement, then shewed our good Lord words full meekly without voice and without opening of lips, right as he had [afore] done, and said full sweetly: "Wit it now well that it was no raving that thou sawest to-day: but take it and believe it, and keep thee therein, and comfort thee therewith, and trust thou thereto: and thou shalt not be overcome."

These last words were said for believing and true sureness that it is our Lord Jesus that shewed me all. And right as in

[1] MS. "enjoyen".

the first word that our good Lord shewed, meaning his blissful Passion—"Herewith is the devil overcome"—right so he said in the last word, with full true secureness, meaning us all: "Thou shalt not be overcome." And all this, believing in this true comfort, it is general, to all mine even-Christians, as it is aforesaid: and so is God's will.

And this word: "Thou shalt not be overcome," was said full clearly[1] and full mightily, for assuredness and comfort against all tribulations that may come. He said not: "Thou shalt not be tempested, thou shalt not be travailed, thou shalt not be dis-eased"; but he said: "Thou shalt not be overcome." God willeth that we take heed to these words, and that we be ever mighty in sure trust, in weal and woe. For he loveth and liketh us, and so willeth he that we love and like him and mightily trust in him; and all shall be well.

And soon after, all was close and I saw no more.


## THE SIXTY-NINTH CHAPTER

Of the second long temptation of the devil to despair;
but she mightily looked to God and to the faith of Holy
Church, rehearsing the Passion of Christ, by the which
she was delivered

AFTER this the Fiend came again with his heat and with his stench, and made me much ado,[2] the stench was so vile and so painful, and also dreadful and travailous. Also I heard a bodily jangling, as if it had been of two persons; and both, to my thinking, jangled at one time as if they had holden a parliament with a great busy-ness; and all was soft muttering, so that I understood naught that they said. And all this was to stir me to despair, as methought—seeming to me

[1] MS. "sharply".      [2] MS. "made me full besy".

as [though] they scorned bidding of beads which are said boisterously with [the] mouth, failing [of] devout attending and wise diligence: the which we owe to God in our prayers.

And our Lord God gave me grace mightily for to trust in him, and to comfort my soul with bodily speech as I should have done to another person that had been travailed. Me-thought that busy-ness[1] might not be likened to no bodily busy-ness. My bodily eye I set in the same Cross where I had been in comfort afore that time; my tongue with speech of Christ's Passion and rehearsing the Faith of Holy Church; and my heart to fasten on God with all the trust and the might. And I thought to myself, meaning: "Thou hast now great busy-ness to keep thee in the Faith for that thou shouldst not be taken of the Enemy: wouldst thou now from this time evermore be so busy to keep thee from sin, this were a good and a sovereign occupation!" For I thought soothly were I safe from sin, I were full safe from all the fiends of hell and enemies of my soul.

And thus he occupied me all that night, and on the morn till it was about prime day. And anon they were all gone, and all passed; and they left nothing but stench, and that lasted still awhile; and I scorned him.

And thus was I delivered from him by the virtue of Christ's Passion: for therewith is the Fiend overcome, as our Lord Jesus Christ said afore.

[1] *Vide supra*, "made me full besy".

## THE SEVENTIETH CHAPTER

In all tribulation we ought to be steadfast in the faith,
trusting mightily in God

IN all this blessed Shewing our good Lord gave understanding that the Sight should pass: which blessed Shewing the
Faith keepeth, with his own good will and his grace. For
he left with me neither sign nor token whereby I might
know it, but he left with me his own blessed word in true
understanding, bidding me full mightily that I should believe it. And so I do—Blessed may he be!—I believe that he
is our Saviour that shewed it, and that it is the Faith that he
shewed: and therefore I believe it, rejoicing. And thereto
I am bounden by all his own meaning, with the next words
that follow: "Keep thee therein, and comfort thee therewith, and trust thou thereto."

Thus I am bounden to keep it in my faith. For on the self
[-same] day that it was shewed, what time that the Sight was
passed, as a wretch I forsook it, and openly I said that I had
raved. Then our Lord Jesus of his mercy would not let it
perish, but he showed it all again within in my soul with
more fulness, with the blessed light of his precious love:
saying these words full mightily and full meekly: "Wit it
now well: it was no raving that thou sawest this day." As if
he had said: "For that the Sight was passed from thee, thou
losedst it and couldst not keep it. But wit it now; that is to
say, now that thou seest it." This was said not only for that
same time, but also to set thereupon the ground of my faith
when he saith anon following: "But take it, believe it, and
keep thee therein and comfort thee therewith and trust
thou thereto; and thou shalt not be overcome."

In these six words that follow, "Take it" [etc.]—his meaning is to fasten it faithfully in our heart: for he willeth that
it dwell with us in faith to our life's end, and after in fulness

143

of joy, willing that we have ever steadfast trust in his blissful behest—knowing his Goodness.

For our faith is contraried in diverse manners by our own blindness, and our ghostly enemy, within and without; and therefore our precious Lover helpeth us with ghostly sight and true teaching in sundry manners within and without, whereby that we may know him. And therefore in what manner he teacheth us, he willeth that we perceive him wisely, receive him sweetly, and keep us in him faithfully. For above the Faith is no goodness kept in this life, as to my sight, and beneath the Faith is no help of soul; but in the Faith, there willeth the Lord that we keep us. For we have by his goodness and his own working to keep us in the Faith; and by his sufferance through ghostly enmity we are assayed in the Faith and made mighty. For if our faith had none enmity, it should deserve no meed, according to the understanding that I have in all our Lord's meaning.

## THE SEVENTY-FIRST CHAPTER

Jesus willeth our soul to be in good cheer to him; and how he sheweth us three manner of cheer

GLAD and merry and sweet is the blissful lovely Cheer of our Lord to our souls. For he heedeth us ever, living in love-longing: and he willeth that our soul be in glad cheer to him, to give him his meed. And thus, I hope, with his grace he hath [drawn], and more shall draw, the Outer Cheer to the Inner Cheer, and make us all one with him, and each of us with other, in true lasting joy that is Jesus.

I have meaning of Three manner of Cheer of our Lord. The first is Cheer of Passion, as he shewed while he was here in this life, dying. Though this [manner of] Beholding be mourning and sorrowful, yet it is glad and merry: for he is God. The second manner of Cheer is [of] Pity and Ruth and Compassion: and this sheweth he, with sureness of Keeping, to all his lovers that hold to his mercy. The third is the Blissful Cheer, as it shall be without end: and this was [shewed] oftenest and longest-continued.

And thus in the time of our pain and our woe he sheweth us Cheer of his Passion and his Cross, helping us to bear [it] by his own blessed virtue. And in the time of our sinning he sheweth to us Cheer of Ruth and Pity, mightily keeping us and defending against all our enemies. And these two be the common Cheer which he sheweth to us in this life; therewith mingling the third: and that is his Blissful Cheer, like, in part, as it shall be in heaven. And that [shewing is] by gracious touching and sweet lighting of the ghostly life, whereby that we are kept in sure faith, hope, and charity, with contrition and devotion, and also with contemplation and all manner of true solace and sweet comforts.

## THE SEVENTY-SECOND CHAPTER

### Sin in the chosen souls is deadly for a time, but they be not dead in the sight of God

But now behoveth me to tell in what manner I saw sin deadly in the creatures which shall not die for sin, but live in the joy of God without end.

I saw that two contrary things should never be together[1] in one place.[2] The most contrary that are, is the highest bliss and the deepest pain. The highest bliss that is, is to have him in clarity of endless life, him verily seeing, him sweetly feeling, all-perfectly having in fulness of joy. And

[1] MS. "to God".     [2] MS. "stede".

thus was the Blissful Cheer of our Lord shewed in Pity: in which Shewing I saw that sin is most contrary—so far forth that as long as we be meddling with any part of sin, we shall never see clearly the Blissful Cheer of our Lord. And the horribler and grievouser that our sins be, the deeper are we for that time from this blissful sight. And therefore it seemeth to us oftentimes as we were in peril of death, in a part of hell, for the sorrow and pain that the sin is to us. And thus we are dead for the time from the very sight of our blissful life. But in all this I saw soothfastly that we be not dead in the sight of God, nor he passeth never from us. But he shall never have his full bliss in us till we have our full bliss in him, verily seeing his fair Blissful Cheer. For we are ordained thereto in kind, and get thereto by grace. Thus I saw how sin is deadly for a short time in the blessed creatures of endless life.

And ever the more clearly that the soul seeth this Blissful Cheer by grace of loving, the more it longeth to see it in fulness. For notwithstanding that our Lord God dwelleth in us and is here with us, and albeit he claspeth us and encloseth us for tender love that he may never leave us, and is more near to us than tongue can tell or heart can think, yet may we never stint of moaning nor of weeping nor of longing till when we see him clearly in his Blissful Cheer. For in that precious blissful sight there may no woe abide, nor any weal fail.

And in this I saw matter of mirth and matter of moaning; matter of mirth: for our Lord, our Maker, is so near to us, and in us, and we in Him, by sureness of keeping through his great goodness; matter of moaning: for our ghostly eye is so blind and we be so borne down by weight of our mortal[1] flesh and darkness of sin, that we may not see our Lord God clearly in his fair Blissful Cheer. No; and because of this

[1] MS. "deadly".

146

dimness[1] scarcely we can believe and trust his great love and our sureness of keeping. And therefore it is that I say we may never stint of moaning nor of weeping. This "weeping" meaneth not all in pouring out of tears by our bodily eye, but also to more ghostly understanding. For the kindly desire of our soul is so great and so unmeasurable, that if there were given us for our solace and for our comfort all the nobleness that ever God made in heaven and in earth, and we saw not the fair Blissful Cheer of himself, yet we should not stint of moaning nor ghostly weeping, that is to say, of painful longing, till when we [should] see verily the fair Blissful Cheer of our Maker. And if we were in all the pain that heart can think and tongue may tell, if we might in that time see his fair Blissful Cheer, all this pain should us not aggrieve.

Thus is that Blissful Sight [the] end of all manner of pain to the loving soul, and the fulfilling of all manner of joy and bliss. And that shewed he in the high, marvellous words where he said: "I it am that is highest; I it am that is lowest; I it am that is all."

It belongeth to us to have three manner of knowings: the first is that we know our Lord God; the second is that we know our self: what we are by him in kind and grace; the third is that we know meekly what our self is anent our sin and feebleness. And for these three was all the Shewing made, as to mine understanding.

[1] MS. "myrkehede, unethes we can leven and trowen".

## THE SEVENTY-THIRD CHAPTER

Of two ghostly sicknesses, of which God willeth that
we amend us, remembering his Passion, knowing also
that he is all love

ALL the blessed teaching of our Lord was shewed by three
parts: that is to say, by bodily sight, and by word formed in
mine understanding, and by ghostly sight. For the bodily
sight, I have said as I saw, as truly as I can; and for the words,
I have said them right as our Lord shewed them to me; and
for the ghostly sight, I have said some deal, but I may never
fully tell it: and therefore of this sight I am stirred to say
more, as God will give me grace.

God shewed two manners of sickness that we have: the
one is impatience, or sloth: for we bear our travail and our
pains heavily; the other is despair, or doubtful dread, as I
shall say of after. Generally, he shewed sin, wherein that all
is comprehended, but in special he shewed not but these
two [only]. And these two are they that most do travail and
tempest us, as by that which our Lord shewed me; and of
them he willeth that we be amended. I speak of such men
and women as for God's love hate sin and dispose themselves to do God's will: then by our ghostly blindness and
bodily heaviness we are most inclining to these. And therefore it is God's will that they be known, for then we shall
refuse them as we do other sins.

And for help of this, full meekly our Lord shewed the
patience that he had in his hard Passion; and also the joying
and the liking that he hath of that Passion, for love. And
this he shewed in example that we should gladly and wisely
bear our pains, for that is great pleasing to him and endless
profit to us. And the cause why we are travailed with them
is for unknowing of Love. Though the three Persons in the

Trinity be all even[1] in Itself, the soul[2] took most understanding in Love; yea, and he willeth that in all things that we have our beholding and our enjoying in Love. And of this knowing are we most blind. For some of us believe that God is Almighty and may do all, and that he is All-Wisdom and can do all; but that he is All-Love and will do all, there we stop short.[3] And this unknowing it is, that letteth most God's lovers, as to my sight.

For when we begin to hate sin, and amend us by the ordinance of Holy Church, yet there dwelleth a dread that letteth us, because of the beholding of our self and of our sins afore done. And some of us because of our every-daily sins: for we hold not our Covenants, nor keep we our cleanness that our Lord setteth us in, but fall oftentimes into so much wretchedness that shame it is to see it. And the beholding of this maketh us so sorry and so heavy, that scarcely we can find any comfort.

And this dread we take sometime for a meekness, but it is a foul blindness and a weakness. And we cannot despise it as we do another sin, that we know [as sin]: for it cometh [subtly] of Enmity, and it is against truth. For of all the properties of the blissful Trinity it is God's will that we should have most sureness and liking in Love: for Love maketh Might and Wisdom full meek to us. For right as by the courtesy of God he forgiveth our sin after the time that we repent us, right so willeth he that we forgive our sin, as anent our unskilful heaviness and our doubtful dreads.

[1] i.e., equal.        [2] i.e., Julian herself.        [3] MS. "astynten".

## THE SEVENTY-FOURTH CHAPTER

There be four manner of dreads: but reverent dread is
a lovely fear that never is without meek love, and yet
they be not both one

FOR I understand [that there be] four manner of dreads. One
is the dread of an affright that cometh to a man suddenly by
frailty. This dread doeth good, for it helpeth to purge man,
as doth bodily sickness or such other pain as is not sin. For
all such pains help man if they be patiently taken. The
second is dread of pain, whereby man is stirred and wakened
from sleep of sin. He is not able for the time to perceive the
soft comfort of the Holy Ghost, till he have understanding
of this dread of pain, of bodily death, of ghostly enemies;
and this dread stirreth us to seek comfort and mercy of God,
and thus this dread helpeth us, and enableth us to have contrition by the blissful touching of the Holy Ghost. The third
is doubtful dread. Doubtful dread, in as much as it draweth
to despair, God will have it turned in us into love by the
knowing of love: that is to say, that the bitterness of doubt
be turned into the sweetness of kind love by grace. For it
may never please our Lord that his servants doubt in his
Goodness. The fourth is reverent dread: for there is no
dread that fully pleaseth God in us but reverent dread. And
that is full soft, for the more it is had, the less it is felt for
sweetness of love.

Love and Dread are brethren, and they are rooted in us
by the Goodness of our Maker, and they shall never be taken
from us without end. We have of kind to love and we have
of grace to love: and we have of kind to dread and we have
of grace to dread. It belongeth to the Lordship and to the
Fatherhood to be dreaded, as it belongeth to the Goodness
to be loved: and it belongeth to us that are his servants and

his children to dread him for Lordship and Fatherhood, as it belongeth to us to love him for Goodness.

And though this reverent dread and love be not parted asunder, yet they are not both one, but they are two in property and in working, and neither of them may be had without other. Therefore I am sure, he that loveth, he dreadeth, though that he feel it but a little.

All dreads other than reverent dread that are proffered to us, though they come under the colour of holiness yet are not so true, and hereby may they be known asunder.— That dread that maketh us hastily to flee from all that is not good and fall into our Lord's breast, as the Child into the Mother's bosom, with all our intent and with all our mind, knowing our feebleness and our great need, knowing his everlasting goodness and his blissful love, only seeking to him for salvation, cleaving to [him] with sure trust: that dread that bringeth us into this working, it is kind, gracious, good, and true. And all that is contrary to this, either it is wrong, or it is mingled with wrong. Then is this the remedy, to know them both and refuse the wrong.

For the kind profit of dread which we have in this life by the gracious working of the Holy Ghost, the same shall be in heaven afore God, gentle, courteous, and full delectable. And thus we shall in love be homely and near to God, and we shall in dread be gentle and courteous to God: and both alike equal.[1]

Desire we of our Lord God to dread him reverently, to love him meekly, to trust in him mightily; for when we dread him reverently and love him meekly our trust is never in vain. For the more that we trust, and the more mightily, the more we please and worship our Lord that we trust in. And if we fail in this reverent dread and meek love (as God forbid we should!), our trust shall soon be misruled for the

[1] MS. "even".

time. And therefore it needeth us much for to pray our Lord of grace that we may have this reverent dread and meek love, of his gift, in heart and in work. For without this, no man may please God.

## THE SEVENTY-FIFTH CHAPTER

### Us needeth love, longing, and pity. Of three manners of longing in God which are in us

I saw that God can do all that we need. And these three that I shall say, we need: love, longing, pity. Pity in love keepeth us in the time of our need; and longing in the same love draweth us into heaven. For the Thirst of God is to have the general Man into him: in which thirst he hath drawn his Holy [ones] that be now in bliss; and getting his lively members, ever he draweth and drinketh, and yet he thirsteth and longeth.

I saw three manners of longing in God, and all to one end; of which we have the same in us, and of the same virtue and for the same end.

The first is, that he longeth to teach us to know him and love him evermore, as it is convenient and speedful to us. The second is, that he longeth to have us up to his Bliss, as souls are when they are taken out of pain into heaven. The third is to fulfil us in bliss; and that shall be on the Last Day, fulfilled ever to last. For I saw, as it is known in our Faith, that the pain and the sorrow shall be ended to all that shall be saved. And not only we shall receive the same bliss that souls afore have had in heaven, but also we shall receive a new [bliss], which plenteously shall be flowing out of God into us and shall fulfil us; and these be the goods which he hath ordained to give us from without beginning. These goods are treasured and hid in himself; for unto that time [no] Creature is mighty nor worthy to receive them.

In this [fulfilling] we shall see verily the cause of all things [that] he hath done; and evermore we shall see the cause of all things that he hath suffered. And the bliss and the fulfilling shall be so deep and so high that, for wonder and marvel, all creatures shall have to God so great reverent dread, overpassing that which hath been seen and felt before, that the pillars of heaven shall tremble and quake. But this manner of trembling and dread shall have no pain; but it belongeth to the worthy might of God thus to be beholden by his creatures, dreadfully trembling and quaking for meekness of joy, marvelling at the greatness of God the Maker and at the littleness of all that is made. For the beholding of this maketh the creature marvellously meek and mild.

Wherefore God willeth—and also it belongeth to us, both in kind and grace—that we wit and know of this, desiring this sight and this working; for it leadeth us in right way, and keepeth us in true life, and oneth us to God. And as good as God is, so great he is; and as much as it belongeth to his goodness to be loved, so much it belongeth to his greatness to be dreaded. For this reverent dread is the fair courtesy that is in Heaven afore God's face. And as much as he shall then be known and loved overpassing that he is now, in so much he shall be dreaded overpassing that he is now. Wherefore it behoveth needs to be that all Heaven and earth shall tremble and quake when the pillars shall tremble and quake.

## THE SEVENTY-SIXTH CHAPTER

A loving soul hateth sin for vileness more than all the
pain of hell: and how the beholding of other men's
sins, unless it be with compassion, letteth the beholding of God

I SPEAK but little of reverent dread, for I hope it may be
seen in this matter aforesaid. But well I wot our Lord
shewed me no souls but those that dread him. For well I
wot the soul that truly taketh the teaching of the Holy
Ghost, it hateth more sin for vileness and horribleness than
it doth all the pain that is in hell. For the soul that beholdeth
the fair kindness of our Lord Jesus, it hateth no hell but sin,
as to my sight. And therefore it is God's will that we know
sin, and pray busily and travail wilfully and seek teaching
meekly that we fall not blindly therein; and if we fall, that
we rise readily. For it is the most pain that the soul may
have, to turn from God any time by sin.

The soul that willeth to be in rest when [an] other man's
sin cometh to mind, he shall flee it as the pain of hell, seeking unto God for remedy, for help against it. For the beholding of [an] other man's sins, it maketh as it were a thick
mist afore the eyes of the soul, and we may not, for the time,
see the fairness of God, unless we may behold them with
contrition with him, with compassion on him, and with
holy desire to God for him. For without this it harmeth[1] and
tempesteth and letteth the soul that beholdeth them. For
this I understood in the Shewing of Compassion.

In this blissful Shewing of our Lord I have understanding
of two contraries: the one is the most wisdom that any
creature may do in this life, the other is the most folly. The
most wisdom is for a creature to do after the will and counsel

[1] MS. "noyith".

of his highest sovereign Friend. This blessed Friend is Jesus, and it is his will and his counsel that we hold us with him, and fasten us to him homely—evermore, in what state soever that we be—for whether-so that we be foul or clean, we are all one in his loving. For weal nor for woe he willeth [that] never we flee from him. But because of the change-ability that we are in, in our self, we fall often into sin. Then we have this [doubting dread] by the stirring of our enemy and by our own folly and blindness : for they say thus : "Thou seest well thou art a wretched creature, a sinner, and also unfaithful.[1] For thou keepest not the Command ; thou dost promise oftentimes our Lord that thou shalt do better, and anon after, thou fallest again into the same, especially into sloth in losing of time." (For that is the beginning of sin, as to my sight—and especially to the creatures that have given them to serve our Lord with inward beholding of his blessed Goodness.) And this maketh us adread to appear afore our courteous Lord. Thus is it our enemy that would put us aback[2] with his false dread, [by reason] of our wretchedness, through pain that he threateth us with. For it is his meaning to make us so heavy and so weary in this, that we should let out of mind the fair, blissful beholding of our Everlasting Friend.

## THE SEVENTY-SEVENTH CHAPTER

Of the enmity of the Fiend, which loseth more in our uprising than he winneth by our falling, and therefore he is scorned

Our good Lord shewed the enmity of the Fiend : whereby I understood that all that is contrary to love and peace is of

---

[1] MS. "ontrewe".        [2] MS. "on bakke".

the Fiend and of his part. And we have, of our feebleness
and our folly, to fall; and we have, of mercy and grace of
the Holy Ghost, to rise to more joy. And if our enemy aught
winneth of us by our falling (for such is his liking), he
loseth manifold more in our rising by charity and meekness.
And this glorious rising, it is to him so great sorrow and
pain for the hate that he hath to our soul, that he burneth
continually in envy. And all this sorrow that he would make
us to have, it shall turn to himself. And for this it was that
our Lord scorned him, and this [it was that] made me mightily to laugh.

Then is this the remedy, that we be aware of our wretchedness and flee to our Lord: for ever the more needy that
we be, the more speedful it is to us to draw nigh to him.[1]
And let us say thus in our meaning: "I know well I have a
shrewd pain; but our Lord is All-Mighty and may punish
me mightily; and he is All-Wisdom and can punish me
skilfully; and he is All-Goodness and loveth me full tenderly." And in this beholding it is necessary for us to abide; for
it is a lovely meekness of a sinful soul, wrought by mercy
and grace of the Holy Ghost, when we wilfully and gladly
take the scourge and chastening of our Lord [that] himself
will give us. And it shall be full tender and full easy, if that
we will only hold us satisfied[2] with him and with all his
works.

For the penance that man taketh of himself was not
shewed me: that is to say, it was not shewed specified. But
specially and highly and with full lovely cheer was it shewed
that we shall meekly bear and suffer the penance that God
himself giveth us, with mind in his blessed Passion. (For
when we have mind in his blessed Passion, with pity and
love, then we suffer with him like as his friends did that
saw it. And this was shewed in the Thirteenth [Shewing],

[1] MS. "neyghen him".          [2] MS. "paid".

near the beginning, where it speaketh of Pity.) For he saith: "Accuse not [thy]self overdone much, deeming that thy tribulation and thy woe is all for thy fault; for I will not that thou be heavy nor sorrowful indiscreetly. For I tell thee, howsoever thou do, thou shalt have woe. And therefore I will that thou wisely know thy penance; and [thou] shalt soothly see that all thy living is penance profitable."

This place is prison and this life is penance, and in the remedy he willeth that we rejoice. The remedy is that our Lord is with us, keeping and leading into the fulness of joy. For this is an endless joy to us in our Lord's meaning, that he, that shall be our bliss when we are there, he is our keeper while we are here. Our way and our heaven is true love and sure trust; and of this he gave understanding in all [the Shewings] and especially in the Shewing of the Passion where he made me mightily to choose him for my heaven.

Flee we to our Lord and we shall be comforted, touch we him and we shall be made clean, cleave we to him and we shall be secure, and safe from all manner of peril.

For our courteous Lord willeth that we should be as homely with him as heart may think or soul may desire. But [let us] beware that we take not so recklessly this homeliness that we leave courtesy. For our Lord himself is sovereign homeliness, and as homely as he is, so courteous he is: for he is very courteous. And the blessed creatures that shall be in heaven with him without end, he will have them like to himself in all things. And to be like our Lord perfectly, it is our very salvation and our full bliss.

And if we wot not how we shall do all this, desire we of our Lord and he shall teach us: for it is his own good-pleasure and his worship; blessed may he be!

## THE SEVENTY-EIGHTH CHAPTER

Our Lord willeth that we know four manner of goodness that he doeth to us: and how we need the light of grace to know our sin and feebleness

Our Lord of his mercy sheweth us our sin and our feebleness by the sweet gracious light of himself; for our sin is so vile and so horrible that he of his courtesy will not shew it to us but by the light of his grace and mercy. Of four things it is his will that we have knowing: the first is, that he is our Ground from whom we have all our life and our being. The second is, that he keepeth us mightily and mercifully in the time that we are in our sin and among all our enemies, that are full fell upon us; and so much we are in the more peril for [that] we give them occasion thereto, and know not our own need. The third is, how courteously he keepeth us, and maketh us to know that we go amiss. The fourth is, how steadfastly he abideth us and changeth no cheer, for he willeth that we be turned and oned to him in love as he is to us.

And thus by this gracious knowing we may see our sin profitably without despair. For soothly we need to see it, and by the sight we shall be made ashamed of our self and brought down as anent our pride and presumption; for it behoveth us verily to see that of ourselves we are right naught but sin and wretchedness. And thus by the sight of the less that our Lord sheweth us, the more is reckoned[1] which we see not. For he of his courtesy measureth the sight to us; for it is so vile and so horrible that we should not endure to see it as it is. And by this meek knowing thus through contrition and grace we shall be broken from all thing that is not our Lord. And then shall our blessed Saviour perfectly heal us, and one us to him.

[1] MS. (probably) "castid".

This breaking and this healing our Lord meaneth for the general Man. For he that is highest and nearest with God, he may see himself sinful—and needeth to—with me; and I that am the least and lowest of those that shall be saved, I may be comforted with him that is highest: so hath our Lord oned us in charity; [as] where he shewed me that I should sin.

And for joy that I had in beholding of him I attended not readily to that Shewing, and our courteous Lord stopped[1] there and would not further teach me till that he gave me grace and will to attend. And hereby was I learned that though we be highly lifted up into contemplation by the special gift of our Lord, yet it behoveth us therewith to have knowing and sight of our sin and our feebleness. For without this knowing we may not have true meekness, and without this [meekness] we may not be saved.

And afterward, also, I saw that we may not have this knowing of our self; nor of none of all our ghostly enemies: for they will us not so great good. For if it were by their will, we should not see it until our ending day. Then be we greatly beholden to God for that he will himself, for love, shew it to us in time of mercy and grace.

## THE SEVENTY-NINTH CHAPTER

We must be mindful of our sin, and not of our neighbours', but for their help. If we fall we must hastily rise, or else we are greatly unkind to God

ALSO I had in this [Revelation] more understanding. In that he shewed me that I should sin, I took it nakedly to mine own singular person, for I was none otherwise shewed at

[1] MS. "stynte".

that time. But by the high, gracious comfort of our Lord
that followed after, I saw that his meaning was for the
general Man: that is to say, All-Man which is sinful and
shall be unto the last day. Of which Man I am a member, as
I hope, by the mercy of God. For the blessed comfort that
I saw, it is large enough for us all. And here was I learned
that I should see mine own sin, and not other men's sins
but if it may be for comfort and help of mine even-Christians.

And also in this same Shewing where I saw that I should
sin, there was I learned to be in dread for unsureness of myself. For I wot not how I shall fall, nor I know not the
measure nor the greatness of sin; for that would I have wist,
with dread, and thereto I had none answer.

Also our courteous Lord in the same time he shewed full
surely and mightily the endlessness and the unchangeable-
ness of his love; and afterward that, by his great goodness
and his grace inwardly keeping, the love of him and our soul
shall never be disparted in two, without end.

And thus in this dread I have matter of meekness that
saveth me from presumption, and in the blessed Shewing of
Love I have matter of true comfort and of joy that saveth
me from despair. All this homely Shewing of our courteous
Lord, it is a lovely lesson and a sweet, gracious teaching of
himself in comforting of our soul. For he willeth that we
[should] know by the sweetness and homely loving of him,
that all that we see or feel, within or without, which is
contrary to this, is of the enemy and not of God. As thus :—
If we be stirred to be the more reckless of our living or of
the keeping of our hearts because that we have knowing of
this plenteous love, then need we greatly to beware. For
this stirring, if it come, is untrue; and greatly we ought to
hate it, for it all hath no likeness of God's will. And when
that we be fallen, by frailty or blindness, then our courteous
Lord toucheth us and stirreth us and claspeth us; and then

willeth he that we see our wretchedness and meekly bear it a-known.[1] But he willeth not that we abide thus, nor he willeth not that we busy us greatly about our accusing, nor he willeth not that we be wretched over our self;[2] but he willeth that we hastily intend unto him. For he standeth all aloof and abideth us sorrowfully and mournfully till when we come, and hath haste to have us to him. For we are his joy and his delight, and he is our salvation and our life.

When I say he standeth all alone, I leave the speaking of the blessed Company of heaven, and speak of his office and his working here on earth—upon the condition of the Shewing.

## THE EIGHTIETH CHAPTER

By three things God is worshipped and we saved

BY three things man standeth in this life; by which three God is worshipped, and we be speeded, kept, and saved.

The first is, use of man's Reason natural; the second is, common teaching of Holy Church; the third is, inward gracious working of the Holy Ghost. And these three be all of one God: God is the ground of our natural reason; and God, the teaching of Holy Church; and God is the Holy Ghost. And all be sundry gifts to which he willeth that we have great regard, and attend us thereto. For these work in us continually all to God; and these be great things. Of which great things he willeth that we have knowing here as it were in an A B C, that is to say, that we have a little knowing; whereof we shall have fulness in heaven. And that is for to speed us.

We know in our Faith that God alone took our nature, and none but he; and furthermore that Christ alone did all

[1] MS. "ben it aknowen".        [2] MS. "wretchful of our selfe".

the works that belong to our salvation, and none but he;
and right so he alone doeth now the last end: that is to say,
he dwelleth here with us, and ruleth us and governeth us
in this living, and bringeth us to his bliss. And this shall he
do as long as any soul is in earth that shall come to heaven—
and so far forth that if there were no such soul but one, he
should be withal alone till he had brought him up to his
bliss. I believe and understand the ministrations of angels,
as clerks tell us: but it was not shewed me. For himself is
nearest and meekest, highest and lowest, and doeth all.
And not only all that we need, but also he doeth all that is
worshipful, to our joy in heaven.

And where I say that he abideth sorrowfully and moaning,
it meaneth all the true feeling that we have in our self, in
contrition and compassion, and all sorrowing and moaning
that we are not oned with our Lord. And all such that is
speedful, it is Christ in us. And though some of us feel it
seldom, it passeth never from Christ till what time he hath
brought us out of all our woe. For love suffereth never to be
without pity. And what time that we fall into sin and leave
the mind of him and the keeping of our own soul, then
keepeth Christ alone all the charge; and thus standeth he
sorrowfully and moaning.

Then belongeth it to us for reverence and kindness to
turn us hastily to our Lord and leave him not alone. He is
here alone with us all: that is to say, only for us he is here.
And what time I am strange to him by sin, despair or sloth,
then I let my Lord stand alone, in as much as it is in me.
And thus it fareth with us all which be sinners. But though
it be so that we do thus oftentimes, his Goodness suffereth
us never to be alone, but lastingly he is with us, and tenderly
he excuseth us, and ever shieldeth us from blame in his sight.

## THE EIGHTY-FIRST CHAPTER

*This blessed woman saw God in divers manners, but she saw him take no resting place but in man's soul*

OUR Good Lord shewed himself in divers manners both in heaven [and] in earth, but I saw him take no place but in man's soul.

He shewed himself in earth in the sweet Incarnation and in his blissful Passion. And in other manner he shewed himself in earth [as in the Revelation] where I say: "I saw God in a Point."[1] And in another manner he shewed himself in earth thus as it were in pilgrimage: that is to say, he is here with us, leading us, and shall be till when he hath brought us all to his bliss in heaven. He shewed him[self] divers times reigning, as it is aforesaid; but principally in man's soul. He hath taken there his resting-place and his worshipful City: out of which worshipful See he shall never rise nor remove without end.

Marvellous and solemn is the place where the Lord dwelleth,[2] and therefore he willeth that we readily answer to[3] his gracious touching, more rejoicing in his whole love than sorrowing in our often fallings. For it is the most worship to him of anything that we may do, that we live gladly and merrily, for his love, in our penance. For he beholdeth us so tenderly that he seeth all our living [here] a penance: for kind loving [in us] is to him aye-lasting penance in us: which penance he worketh in us, and mercifully he helpeth us to bear it. For his love maketh him to long [for us]; his wisdom and his truth with his rightfulness maketh him to suffer us [to be] here: and in this same manner [of longing and abiding] he willeth to see it in us. For this is our kindly penance—and the highest, as to my sight. For this penance

[1] *Vide supra*, Chap. 11.      [2] MS. "wonneth".      [3] MS. "entenden to".

goeth[1] never from us till what time that we be fulfilled, when we shall have him to our meed. And therefore he willeth that we set our hearts in the Overpassing: that is to say, from the pain that we feel into the bliss that we trust.

## THE EIGHTY-SECOND CHAPTER

### God beholdeth the mourning of the soul with pity and not with blame, and yet we do naught but sin

BUT here shewed our courteous Lord the moaning and the mourning of the soul, meaning thus: "I wot well thou wilt live for my love, merrily and gladly suffering all the penance that may come to thee; but in as much as thou livest not without sin thou wouldest suffer, for my love, all the woe, all the tribulation and dis-ease that might come to thee. And it is sooth. But be not greatly aggrieved with sin that falleth to thee against thy will."

And here I understood that [which was shewed] that the Lord beholdeth the servant with pity and not with blame.[2] For this passing life asketh not to live all without blame and sin. He loveth us endlessly, and we sin customably, and he sheweth us full mildly, and then we sorrow and mourn discreetly, turning us unto the beholding of his mercy, cleaving to his love and goodness, seeing that he is our medicine, witting that we do naught but sin. And thus by the meekness we get by the sight of our sin, faithfully knowing his everlasting love, him thanking and praising, we please him:—"I love thee, and thou lovest me, and our love shall not be disparted in two; for thy profit I suffer [these things to come]." And all this was shewed in ghostly under-

[1] MS. "cometh".          [2] *Vide supra*, Chap 51.

standing, saying these blessed words: "1 keep thee full surely."

And by [the] great desire that I have in our blessed Lord that we shall live in this manner—that is to say, in longing and enjoying, as all this lesson of love sheweth—thereby I understood that all that [which] is contrarious to us is not of him but of enmity; and he willeth that we know it by the sweet gracious light of his kind love. If any such lover be in earth which is continually kept from falling I know it not: for it was not shewed me. But this was shewed: that in falling and in rising we are ever preciously kept in one Love. For in the Beholding of God we fall not, and in the beholding of self we stand not; and both these [manners of beholding] be sooth as to my sight. But the Beholding of our Lord God is the highest soothness. Then are we greatly bound to God [for] that he will in this living shew us this high soothness. And I understood that while we be in this life it is full speedful to us that we see both these at once. For the higher Beholding keepeth us in ghostly solace and true enjoying in God; [and] that other, that is the lower Beholding, keepeth us in dread and maketh us ashamed of ourself. But our good Lord willeth ever that we hold us much more in the Beholding of the higher, and [yet] leave not the knowing of the lower, unto the time that we be brought up above, where we shall have our Lord Jesus unto our meed and be fulfilled of joy and bliss without end.

## THE EIGHTY-THIRD CHAPTER

Of three properties in God, life, love, and light, and
that our reason is in God according

I HAD, in part, touching, sight, and feeling in three properties of God, in which the strength and effect of all the
Revelation standeth: and they were seen in every Shewing,
and most properly in the Twelfth, where it saith oftentimes: ["I it am."] The properties are these: Life, Love, and
Light. In life is marvellous homeliness, and in love is gentle
courtesy, and in light is endless kind-hood. These properties
were in one Goodness: unto which Goodness my Reason
would be oned, and cleave to it with all its might.

I beheld with reverent dread, and highly marvelling in the
sight and in the feeling of the sweet accord, that our Reason
is in God; understanding that it is the highest gift that we
have received; and it is grounded in kind.

Our faith is a light kindly coming of our endless Day, that
is our Father, God. In which light our Mother, Christ, and
our good Lord, the Holy Ghost, leadeth us in this passing
life. This light is measured discreetly, needfully standing to
us in the night. The light is cause of our life; the night is
cause of our pain and of all our woe: in which we deserve
meed and thanks of God. For we, with mercy and grace,
wilfastly know and believe our light, going therein wisely
and mightily.

And at the end of woe, suddenly our eyes shall be opened,
and in clarity of light our sight shall be full: which light is
God, our Maker and Holy Ghost, in Christ Jesus our
Saviour.

Thus I saw and understood that our faith is our light in our
night: which light is God, our endless Day.

## THE EIGHTY-FOURTH CHAPTER

Charity is this light, for faith and hope lead us to charity

THE light is Charity, and the measuring of this light is done to us profitably by the wisdom of God. For neither is the light so large that we may see our blissful Day, nor is it shut[1] from us; but it is such a light in which we may live meedfully, with travail deserving the endless worship of God. And this was seen in the Sixth Shewing where he said: "I thank thee of thy service and of thy travail." Thus Charity keepeth us in Faith and in Hope, and Hope leadeth us in Charity. And at the end all shall be Charity.

I had three manners of understanding in this light, Charity. The first is Charity unmade; the second is Charity made; the third is Charity given. Charity unmade is God; Charity made is our soul in God; Charity given is virtue. And that is a gracious gift of working in which we love God, for himself; and ourselves, in God; and that [which] God loveth, for God.

## THE EIGHTY-FIFTH CHAPTER

God loved his chosen from without beginning. How privities now hidden shall be known in heaven, wherefore we shall bless our Lord that everything is so well ordained

AND in this sight I marvelled highly. For notwithstanding our simple living and our blindness here, yet endlessly our courteous Lord beholdeth us in this working, rejoicing; and of all things, we may please him best wisely and truly

[1] MS. "speñd".

to believe it, and to enjoy with him and in him. For as
verily as we shall be in the bliss of God without end, him
praising and thanking, so verily we have been in the foresight of God, loved and known in his endless purpose from
without beginning. In which unbeginning love he made us;
and in the same love he keepeth us and never suffereth us to
be hurt [in any way] by which our bliss might be lost. And
therefore when the Doom is given and we be all brought up
above, then [shall] we clearly see in God the privities which
now be hidden to us. Then shall none of us be stirred to say
in any wise: "Lord, if it had been thus, then it had been full
well"; but we shall say all with one voice: "Lord, blessed
mayst thou be, for it is thus: it is well; and now see we
verily that all-thing is done as it was then ordained before
that anything was made."

## THE EIGHTY-SIXTH CHAPTER

The good Lord shewed that this book should be otherwise performed than at the first writing; for, fifteen
years after, it was answered that the cause of all this
shewing was love. Which may Jesus grant us. Amen.

THIS book is begun by God's gift and his grace, but it is not
yet performed, as to my sight.

For Charity pray we all to God with God's working,
thanking, trusting, enjoying. For thus will our good Lord
be prayed [to], as by the understanding that I took in all his
own meaning and in the sweet words where he saith full
merrily: "I am the Ground of thy beseeching." For truly I
saw and understood in our Lord's meaning that he shewed
it for that he willeth to have it known more than it is: in
which knowing he will give us grace to love him and cleave

to him. For he beholdeth his heavenly treasure with so great love on earth that he will give us more light and solace in heavenly joy, in drawing [to him] of our hearts, for sorrow and darkness[1] which we are in.

And from that time that it was shewed I desired oftentimes to witten what was our Lord's meaning. And fifteen years after, and more, I was answered in ghostly understanding, saying thus: "Wouldst thou witten thy Lord's meaning in this thing? Wit it well: Love was his meaning. Who shewed it thee? Love. What shewed he thee? Love. Wherefore shewed it he? For Love. Hold thee therein and thou shalt witten and know more in the same. But thou shalt never know nor witten therein other thing without end." Thus was I learned[2] that Love was our Lord's meaning.

And I saw full surely in this and in all, that ere God made us he loved us; which love was never slacked, nor ever shall be. And in this love he hath done all his works; and in this love he hath made all things profitable to us; and in this love our life is everlasting. In our making we had beginning; but the love wherein he made us was in him from without beginning: in which love we have our beginning. And all this shall we see in God, without end. Which may Jesus grant us. Amen.


### [Addition by the Scribe.]

Thus endeth the Revelation of Love of the blessed Trinity shewed by our Saviour Christ Jesus for our endless comfort and solace, and also to enjoy in him in this passing journey of this life.

*Amen, Jesu, Amen.*

---

[1] MS. "merkness" = dimness.      [2] MS. "lerid".

I pray Almighty God that this book come not but to the hands of them that will be his faithful lovers, and to those that will submit them to the faith of holy Church, and obey the wholesome understanding and teaching of the men that be of virtuous life, sad age, and profound learning: for this Revelation is high Divinity and high wisdom, wherefore it may not dwell with him that is thrall to sin and to the Devil.

And beware thou take not one thing after thy affection and liking, and leave another: for that is the condition of a heretic. But take everything with other, and truly understand [that] all is according to holy Scripture and grounded in the same. And that Jesus, our very love, light and truth, shall shew to all clean souls that with meekness ask perseveringly this wisdom of him.

And thou to whom this book shall come, thank highly and heartily our Saviour, Christ Jesus, that he made these shewings and revelations for thee, and to thee, of his endless love, mercy and goodness, for thine and our safe guide, to conduct to everlasting bliss:

The which may Jesus grant us.

Amen.

# NOTES

NOTE 1, p. 4, ll. 22 *et sqq.*

This paragraph appears in the Amherst MS. in a form so different that it will be of interest to print it here. I give the text as modernized by Rev. Dundas Harford, in *The Shewings of Lady Julian*, p. 20.

"As for the third desire, I heard a man tell of Holy Church of the story of Saint Cecilia. In the which showing I understood that she had three wounds in her neck, with the which she pined to death. By the stirring of this I conceived a mighty desire, praying our Lord God that he would grant me three wounds in my lifetime: that is to say, the wound of contrition, the wound of compassion, and the wound of wilful longing towards God. Right as I asked the other two with a condition, so I asked the third without any condition. These two desires beforesaid passed from my mind. And the third dwelled continually."

NOTE 2, p. 33, ll. 29 *et sqq.*

In the Amherst MS. this paragraph reads as follows (Harford, p. 59):

"This showing of Christ's pains filled me full of pains, for I wot well he suffered not but once, but as he would show it me and fill me with mind [of it], as I had desired before. My mother, that stood amongst others and beheld me, lifted up her hand before my face to lock mine eyes, for she weened I had been dead, or else I had died. And this increased much my sorrow, for notwithstanding all my pains, I would not have been letted for love that I had in him; and nevertheless in all this time of Christ's presence I felt no pain but for Christ's pains. Then I thought I knew fully for what pain it was that I asked; for methought that my pains passed any bodily death."

NOTE 3, chap. 32, pp. 55–8.

The language of this chapter with regard to evil, and especially to eternal punishment in hell, is obscure and liable to misunder-

standing, since it might be taken to mean that, at the last day, the
souls of the damned will, in some unexplained manner, attain to
eternal salvation. This, of course, is contrary to Catholic theology,
as Julian herself clearly recognizes (*v.* p. *57*). Her language, however, can be paralleled from the writings of other mystics whose
orthodoxy is above suspicion. The whole question is dealt with in
a masterly way by Father A. B. Sharpe, in Chap. VI of his well-
known work *Mysticism, its True Nature and Value* (London, 1910).
In this he quotes the words of Julian in Chap. 32 and sets beside them a very similar passage from Blessed Angela of Foligno,
which runs as follows:—"I felt myself in such fulness of charity,
and I understood with such joy in that power and will and justice
of God, that I understood not only those things about which I
had asked, but I was satisfied as to the salvation offered to every
creature, and about the devil and the damned and all things. But
all this I cannot explain in words" (Translation of A. Thorold,
*Catholic Mysticism*, p. 141).

The argument underlying these and similar passages in the
writings of the mystics is summarized by Father Sharpe as follows:[1]
"They [the mystics] are agreed that evil—whether considered as
sin or as the suffering consequent upon it—has no substantive
existence; it is the negation of good and no more. There can be
no *Summum Malum*, St Thomas declares, for this reason. As to how
evil comes into being, and what is its place and meaning in a universe that must be considered wholly good, they are by no means
explicit. They know—but they cannot explain how they know—
that evil has no permanence and no substantial reality; that it
neither mars the perfect goodness and omnipotence of God nor
troubles the peace of those who are united with him—that in the
end all will somehow be perfectly well. This no doubt is quite
satisfactory to the mystic who receives the supernatural assurance;
but it is hardly applicable by way of argument or explanation to
the perplexities of others in this matter.

"Nevertheless, it is quite possible to construct a theodicy, or
vindication of the divine justice, upon the principle which lies
at the root of supernatural mysticism. Indeed, it is scarcely pos-

[1] Op. cit., p. 123 f.

sible to do so in any other way. That principle, as we have seen, is the absoluteness, or the infinite perfection and independence of the divine nature. All depends upon God, but he himself on nothing but himself. Consequently, his motive in creating is in himself—his own 'glory' or 'pleasure'; and this is the only absolutely good motive which can be conceived for any action on the part of either the Creator or the creature. But if God is 'glorified' by the creation of this world; if his power and justice are manifested in the reward of the good and the punishment of the wicked; then certainly the act of creation is good, its motive is fulfilled. Evil is the work of the creature, not of the Creator, whose justice and mercy alike it is the means of exhibiting.

"Further, the goodness of the act of creation is not vitiated by the fact that it involves the self-caused misery, temporal or eternal, of the human race. At first sight this does appear to be a grave difficulty, in the way of reconciling omnipotence with perfect goodness; for, it is asked, if God could create a world in which no evil could exist, or could even abstain from creating this one, why did he not do so? Or if he could not do either, how can he be omnipotent? But evil is the work of created free-will, not of God; if, therefore, God had abstained from the creation of this world (or what is the same thing, had made it different) because of man's actions foreseen either as possible or as certain, then God would not have acted as God, but in contravention of his very nature. There would have been a corner of the possible universe from which he would have been excluded, a good act which he might not do; he would have been limited by and dependent on the free actions of his possible creatures. But such an idea is inconceivable: God cannot at the same time be perfect and limited, or dependent and independent, or supreme and subject to the will of his creatures; and if he could act in subordination to anything external to himself, he would no longer exist—he would have destroyed himself. To remove the centre of a circle is to destroy both centre and circle, and if God were not the centre of the circle of the universe, neither he nor it could exist.

"Thus the difficulty of reconciling the existence of evil with the omnipotence and goodness of a divine creator disappears as soon as the essential nature of God is realized in respect of its independence and supremacy."

The whole chapter should be read; it is a wonderfully convincing exposition of the mystical solution of the whole problem of evil.

NOTE 4, p. 66, l. 8.

*Cf.* St Bernard, *in Cant. Serm.* xxiii 15: "The purpose of God standeth firm: the judgement of peace standeth firm over them that fear him, hiding their evil deeds and recording their good: so that, in a wondrous manner, not only good but also evil things work together for good to them. O truly and only *Blessed is he to whom the Lord will not impute sin.* For no one is there who hath not had sin. For *all have sinned*, and all *have need of the glory of God.* Yet *who shall accuse against the elect of God?* It is enough for me for all justification to have only him propitious against whom I have sinned. For all that he has decreed not to impute to me is as though it had not been. Not to sin is the justice of God: the justice of man is the pardon of God. I have seen these things, and I have understood the truth of that sentence: *Every one who is born of God sinneth not, because the heavenly generation preserveth him.* The heavenly generation is eternal predestination, by which God hath loved his elect, and made them acceptable in his beloved Son before the foundation of the world, so that in the sanctuary they may come before him, to see his power and his glory, when they shall be made partakers of his inheritance, and shall appear conformed to his likeness. These then I have marked as never having sinned. Because, although they seem in some sort to have fallen, they do not appear so in eternity, for the charity of the Father covereth the multitude of their sins."

I owe this reference and translation to the Rev. H. Collins' edition of the *Revelations* (London, 1877).

[Closer parallels to the teaching of Dame Julian may be found in the writings of a great friend of St Bernard's, Abbot William of St Thierry. See especially Section 61 of his *Epistle to the Brethren of*

*Mont Dieu* (London, 1930). The Introduction to that English translation discusses the doctrine at some length. Abbot William has the same teaching in another treatise of his, and on that occasion crystallizes his opinion in the proposition: "Peter when he sinned did not lose charity." St Thomas in his *Secunda Secundae* (Q. xxiv, Art. 12), having asked other questions about charity, inquires whether it is lost by one act of mortal sin and answers with an emphatic affirmative. It is impossible, he holds, that the infused virtue of charity, so supernatural and even divine in its character, should co-exist in a soul with serious sin. Against this view he produces Abbot William's proposition regarding St Peter, but has no difficulty in disposing of it. Abbot William belongs to the twelfth century and his teaching on this point may be regarded as one of those pre-scholastic opinions which were inevitably dismissed when the great scholastics worked out their scientific theology. But Abbot William's writings remained in circulation and since they were very commonly ascribed to St Bernard obtained all the authority of that great name. It seems probable that they are the ultimate source of Dame Julian's doctrine.]

NOTE 5, p. 118, l. 15.

On this chapter Fr. H. Collins has the following valuable Note.

By the word *substance* is to be understood the soul, considered in its *spiritual* nature and higher faculties. By the *sensuality* is meant the soul as knit to a *fleshly* nature, and affected by it. The *substance* or spirit is joined to Christ by the tie of fatherhood, because he, as God, created it. The sensuality or flesh, transmitted by Adam, became united to him when he, the Word, became Incarnate. This union is handed on to the members of his Church by Baptism and the Holy Eucharist. Christ thus knits to him the whole man—the spirit and the fleshly nature, the substance and the sensuality.

# GLOSSARY

*Adight:* prepared, disposed.

*Adventure:* chance, hazard, risk.

*After:* according to.

*All thing:* with a singular verb—generally for *all*, the *whole*; sometimes for *every*, *each*. In Early and Middle English *thing* had no *s* in the plural.

*And:* sometimes for *but*, more rarely in the sense of *if*, *and though*, *and when*.

*Asketh:* requireth.

*Asseth, asyeth, asyeth-making:* satisfaction, atonement.

*Avisement:* attention.

*Beclosed:* enclosed.

*Behest:* promise; more rarely command.

*Behold in:* behold. *Beholding:* way of regarding things.

*Belongeth to, behoveth:* is incumbent on, befitteth.

*Blissful:* used sometimes for *blessed*.

*Blyn:* cease.

*Bodily:* perceived by any of the bodily senses.

*Braste:* burst.

*Busyness:* the state of being busy.

*But if:* unless.

*Buxom:* obedient, submissive.

*Cause:* reason, end, motive.

*Cheer:* expression of countenance shewing sorrow, gladness, etc.

*Close:* shut away; hid, or partially hid.

*Come from:* go from.

*Contrarious:* perverse.

*Could* and *can* often as referring to knowledge and ability.

*Courteous:* gentle, reverentially ceremonious, gracious.

*Deadly:* mortal.

*Dearworthy:* precious, loved and honoured.

*Depart:* dispart, separate.

*Deserve:* earn.

# GLOSSARY

*Dis-ease:* lack of ease, distress.

*Doom, deeming:* judgement. *Doomsman:* confessor.

*Enjoy in:* enjoy, rejoice in.

*Entend:* attend.

*Enter:* to lead in.

*Even:* equal; *even-like, even-right:* straight, straight-facing.

*Even-Christian:* fellow-Christian.

*For that:* because.

*Fulfilled of:* filled full with. *Fulfilling:* fulfilment.

*Fulsomely:* most fully.

*Garland:* crown (of thorns).

*Generally:* relating to things or people in general, not individually.

*Ghostly:* spiritual, spiritually.

*Gramercy:* "grand merci," great thanks.

*Hastily:* quickly, soon.

*Have to:* betake oneself to.

*Homely:* intimate, simple, "at home."

*Honest:* fair, seemly.

*Impropriated, impropried to:* appropriated, assigned to.

*Indifferent:* indistinct.

*Intellect:* understanding, meaning.

*Intent:* attention.

*Kind:* (subs.) nature, species; (adj.) natural.

*Kindly:* natural, filial; also in modern sense, gentle, genial, human.

*Known:* made known.

*Langour:* to languish.

*Learn:* teach.

*Let:* hinder (*letted:* hindered).

*Like (it liketh him, meliketh):* to suit, to be pleasing.

*Liking:* pleasure.

*Likeness* ("without any likeness"): comparison.

*May, might:* often for modern *can* and *could*.

*Mean:* to think, say, intend, to have in mind.

*Mean, means:* medium, intermediary.

*Mights:* powers, faculties.

*Mind:* feeling, memory, perception.

*Mischief:* hurt, injury.

# GLOSSARY

*Naked:* simple, single, by itself.

*Needs:* of need; *it behoveth needs:* must of necessity.

*One, oned, oneing:* to make one, unite.

*Over:* upper.

*Overpassing:* exceeding.

*Oweth:* ought, is bound by duty.

*Pass:* to die.

*Passing:* surpassingly.

*Ready:* prepared; *readily:* quickly.

*Regard:* (subs.) look, sight.

*Regard, in regard of:* in respect of, comparison with.

*Sad:* sober, serious.

*Sadly:* soberly, seriously.

*Say:* tell.

*Siker:* secure, sure.

*Sikerness:* security, sureness.

*Skilfully:* discerningly.

*Slade:* a steep, narrow place; a ravine.

*So far forth:* to such a measure.

*Solemn:* festal; *solemnly:* stately, ceremonially.

*Sooth:* very truth, that which *is; soothly, soothfastly, soothfastness.*

*Speed:* profit, advance.

*Stint:* to cease.

*Stirring:* moving, prompting to action.

*Substance* and *sensuality:* see Note 4, *supra.*

*Tarry:* to vex, delay.

*Touch* (a): an instant. *Touching:* influence.

*Trow:* believe.

*Unknowing:* ignorance.

*Unmade:* not made.

*Ween:* think, suppose.

*Will; He will:* He willeth that.

*Wilfully:* with firm will, resolutely.

*Wit:* to know by perception, to experience, find, learn.

*Worship:* honour, praise, glory.

*Wretch:* a poor creature, one of no account.

A CATALOG OF SELECTED
# DOVER BOOKS
IN ALL FIELDS OF INTEREST

# A CATALOG OF SELECTED DOVER
# BOOKS IN ALL FIELDS OF INTEREST

100 BEST-LOVED POEMS, Edited by Philip Smith. "The Passionate Shepherd to His Love," "Shall I compare thee to a summer's day?" "Death, be not proud," "The Raven," "The Road Not Taken," plus works by Blake, Wordsworth, Byron, Shelley, Keats, many others. 96pp. 5³⁄₁₆ x 8¼. 0-486-28553-7

100 SMALL HOUSES OF THE THIRTIES, Brown-Blodgett Company. Exterior photographs and floor plans for 100 charming structures. Illustrations of models accompanied by descriptions of interiors, color schemes, closet space, and other amenities. 200 illustrations. 112pp. 8⅜ x 11. 0-486-44131-8

1000 TURN-OF-THE-CENTURY HOUSES: With Illustrations and Floor Plans, Herbert C. Chivers. Reproduced from a rare edition, this showcase of homes ranges from cottages and bungalows to sprawling mansions. Each house is meticulously illustrated and accompanied by complete floor plans. 256pp. 9⅜ x 12¼.
0-486-45596-3

101 GREAT AMERICAN POEMS, Edited by The American Poetry & Literacy Project. Rich treasury of verse from the 19th and 20th centuries includes works by Edgar Allan Poe, Robert Frost, Walt Whitman, Langston Hughes, Emily Dickinson, T. S. Eliot, other notables. 96pp. 5³⁄₁₆ x 8¼. 0-486-40158-8

101 GREAT SAMURAI PRINTS, Utagawa Kuniyoshi. Kuniyoshi was a master of the warrior woodblock print — and these 18th-century illustrations represent the pinnacle of his craft. Full-color portraits of renowned Japanese samurais pulse with movement, passion, and remarkably fine detail. 112pp. 8⅜ x 11. 0-486-46523-3

ABC OF BALLET, Janet Grosser. Clearly worded, abundantly illustrated little guide defines basic ballet-related terms: arabesque, battement, pas de chat, relevé, sissonne, many others. Pronunciation guide included. Excellent primer. 48pp. 4³⁄₁₆ x 5¾.
0-486-40871-X

ACCESSORIES OF DRESS: An Illustrated Encyclopedia, Katherine Lester and Bess Viola Oerke. Illustrations of hats, veils, wigs, cravats, shawls, shoes, gloves, and other accessories enhance an engaging commentary that reveals the humor and charm of the many-sided story of accessorized apparel. 644 figures and 59 plates. 608pp. 6⅛ x 9¼.
0-486-43378-1

ADVENTURES OF HUCKLEBERRY FINN, Mark Twain. Join Huck and Jim as their boyhood adventures along the Mississippi River lead them into a world of excitement, danger, and self-discovery. Humorous narrative, lyrical descriptions of the Mississippi valley, and memorable characters. 224pp. 5³⁄₁₆ x 8¼. 0-486-28061-6

ALICE STARMORE'S BOOK OF FAIR ISLE KNITTING, Alice Starmore. A noted designer from the region of Scotland's Fair Isle explores the history and techniques of this distinctive, stranded-color knitting style and provides copious illustrated instructions for 14 original knitwear designs. 208pp. 8⅜ x 10⅞. 0-486-47218-3

Browse over 9,000 books at www.doverpublications.com

ALICE'S ADVENTURES IN WONDERLAND, Lewis Carroll. Beloved classic about a little girl lost in a topsy-turvy land and her encounters with the White Rabbit, March Hare, Mad Hatter, Cheshire Cat, and other delightfully improbable characters. 42 illustrations by Sir John Tenniel. 96pp. 5³⁄₁₆ x 8¼. 0-486-27543-4

AMERICA'S LIGHTHOUSES: An Illustrated History, Francis Ross Holland. Profusely illustrated fact-filled survey of American lighthouses since 1716. Over 200 stations — East, Gulf, and West coasts, Great Lakes, Hawaii, Alaska, Puerto Rico, the Virgin Islands, and the Mississippi and St. Lawrence Rivers. 240pp. 8 x 10¾.
0-486-25576-X

AN ENCYCLOPEDIA OF THE VIOLIN, Alberto Bachmann. Translated by Frederick H. Martens. Introduction by Eugene Ysaye. First published in 1925, this renowned reference remains unsurpassed as a source of essential information, from construction and evolution to repertoire and technique. Includes a glossary and 73 illustrations. 496pp. 6½ x 9¼. 0-486-46618-3

ANIMALS: 1,419 Copyright-Free Illustrations of Mammals, Birds, Fish, Insects, etc., Selected by Jim Harter. Selected for its visual impact and ease of use, this outstanding collection of wood engravings presents over 1,000 species of animals in extremely lifelike poses. Includes mammals, birds, reptiles, amphibians, fish, insects, and other invertebrates. 284pp. 9 x 12. 0-486-23766-4

THE ANNALS, Tacitus. Translated by Alfred John Church and William Jackson Brodribb. This vital chronicle of Imperial Rome, written by the era's great historian, spans A.D. 14-68 and paints incisive psychological portraits of major figures, from Tiberius to Nero. 416pp. 5³⁄₁₆ x 8¼. 0-486-45236-0

ANTIGONE, Sophocles. Filled with passionate speeches and sensitive probing of moral and philosophical issues, this powerful and often-performed Greek drama reveals the grim fate that befalls the children of Oedipus. Footnotes. 64pp. 5³⁄₁₆ x 8 ¼. 0-486-27804-2

ART DECO DECORATIVE PATTERNS IN FULL COLOR, Christian Stoll. Reprinted from a rare 1910 portfolio, 160 sensuous and exotic images depict a breathtaking array of florals, geometrics, and abstracts — all elegant in their stark simplicity. 64pp. 8⅜ x 11. 0-486-44862-2

THE ARTHUR RACKHAM TREASURY: 86 Full-Color Illustrations, Arthur Rackham. Selected and Edited by Jeff A. Menges. A stunning treasury of 86 full-page plates span the famed English artist's career, from *Rip Van Winkle* (1905) to masterworks such as *Undine, A Midsummer Night's Dream,* and *Wind in the Willows* (1939). 96pp. 8⅜ x 11.
0-486-44685-9

THE AUTHENTIC GILBERT & SULLIVAN SONGBOOK, W. S. Gilbert and A. S. Sullivan. The most comprehensive collection available, this songbook includes selections from every one of Gilbert and Sullivan's light operas. Ninety-two numbers are presented uncut and unedited, and in their original keys. 410pp. 9 x 12.
0-486-23482-7

THE AWAKENING, Kate Chopin. First published in 1899, this controversial novel of a New Orleans wife's search for love outside a stifling marriage shocked readers. Today, it remains a first-rate narrative with superb characterization. New introductory Note. 128pp. 5³⁄₁₆ x 8¼. 0-486-27786-0

BASIC DRAWING, Louis Priscilla. Beginning with perspective, this commonsense manual progresses to the figure in movement, light and shade, anatomy, drapery, composition, trees and landscape, and outdoor sketching. Black-and-white illustrations throughout. 128pp. 8⅜ x 11. 0-486-45815-6

THE BATTLES THAT CHANGED HISTORY, Fletcher Pratt. Historian profiles 16 crucial conflicts, ancient to modern, that changed the course of Western civilization. Gripping accounts of battles led by Alexander the Great, Joan of Arc, Ulysses S. Grant, other commanders. 27 maps. 352pp. 5⅜ x 8½.                    0-486-41129-X

BEETHOVEN'S LETTERS, Ludwig van Beethoven. Edited by Dr. A. C. Kalischer. Features 457 letters to fellow musicians, friends, greats, patrons, and literary men. Reveals musical thoughts, quirks of personality, insights, and daily events. Includes 15 plates. 410pp. 5⅜ x 8½.                    0-486-22769-3

BERNICE BOBS HER HAIR AND OTHER STORIES, F. Scott Fitzgerald. This brilliant anthology includes 6 of Fitzgerald's most popular stories: "The Diamond as Big as the Ritz," the title tale, "The Offshore Pirate," "The Ice Palace," "The Jelly Bean," and "May Day." 176pp. 5⅜ x 8½.                    0-486-47049-0

BESLER'S BOOK OF FLOWERS AND PLANTS: 73 Full-Color Plates from Hortus Eystettensis, 1613, Basilius Besler. Here is a selection of magnificent plates from the *Hortus Eystettensis,* which vividly illustrated and identified the plants, flowers, and trees that thrived in the legendary German garden at Eichstätt. 80pp. 8⅜ x 11.
0-486-46005-3

THE BOOK OF KELLS, Edited by Blanche Cirker. Painstakingly reproduced from a rare facsimile edition, this volume contains full-page decorations, portraits, illustrations, plus a sampling of textual leaves with exquisite calligraphy and ornamentation. 32 full-color illustrations. 32pp. 9⅜ x 12¼.                    0-486-24345-1

THE BOOK OF THE CROSSBOW: With an Additional Section on Catapults and Other Siege Engines, Ralph Payne-Gallwey. Fascinating study traces history and use of crossbow as military and sporting weapon, from Middle Ages to modern times. Also covers related weapons: balistas, catapults, Turkish bows, more. Over 240 illustrations. 400pp. 7¼ x 10⅛.                    0-486-28720-3

THE BUNGALOW BOOK: Floor Plans and Photos of 112 Houses, 1910, Henry L. Wilson. Here are 112 of the most popular and economic blueprints of the early 20th century — plus an illustration or photograph of each completed house. A wonderful time capsule that still offers a wealth of valuable insights. 160pp. 8⅜ x 11.
0-486-45104-6

THE CALL OF THE WILD, Jack London. A classic novel of adventure, drawn from London's own experiences as a Klondike adventurer, relating the story of a heroic dog caught in the brutal life of the Alaska Gold Rush. Note. 64pp. 5³⁄₁₆ x 8¼.
0-486-26472-6

CANDIDE, Voltaire. Edited by Francois-Marie Arouet. One of the world's great satires since its first publication in 1759. Witty, caustic skewering of romance, science, philosophy, religion, government — nearly all human ideals and institutions. 112pp. 5³⁄₁₆ x 8¼.                    0-486-26689-3

CELEBRATED IN THEIR TIME: Photographic Portraits from the George Grantham Bain Collection, Edited by Amy Pastan. With an Introduction by Michael Carlebach. Remarkable portrait gallery features 112 rare images of Albert Einstein, Charlie Chaplin, the Wright Brothers, Henry Ford, and other luminaries from the worlds of politics, art, entertainment, and industry. 128pp. 8⅜ x 11.                    0-486-46754-6

CHARIOTS FOR APOLLO: The NASA History of Manned Lunar Spacecraft to 1969, Courtney G. Brooks, James M. Grimwood, and Loyd S. Swenson, Jr. This illustrated history by a trio of experts is the definitive reference on the Apollo spacecraft and lunar modules. It traces the vehicles' design, development, and operation in space. More than 100 photographs and illustrations. 576pp. 6¾ x 9¼. 0-486-46756-2

A CHRISTMAS CAROL, Charles Dickens. This engrossing tale relates Ebenezer Scrooge's ghostly journeys through Christmases past, present, and future and his ultimate transformation from a harsh and grasping old miser to a charitable and compassionate human being. 80pp. 5‰₆ x 8¼. 0-486-26865-9

COMMON SENSE, Thomas Paine. First published in January of 1776, this highly influential landmark document clearly and persuasively argued for American separation from Great Britain and paved the way for the Declaration of Independence. 64pp. 5‰₆ x 8¼. 0-486-29602-4

THE COMPLETE SHORT STORIES OF OSCAR WILDE, Oscar Wilde. Complete texts of "The Happy Prince and Other Tales," "A House of Pomegranates," "Lord Arthur Savile's Crime and Other Stories," "Poems in Prose," and "The Portrait of Mr. W. H." 208pp. 5‰₆ x 8¼. 0-486-45216-6

COMPLETE SONNETS, William Shakespeare. Over 150 exquisite poems deal with love, friendship, the tyranny of time, beauty's evanescence, death, and other themes in language of remarkable power, precision, and beauty. Glossary of archaic terms. 80pp. 5‰₆ x 8¼. 0-486-26686-9

THE COUNT OF MONTE CRISTO: Abridged Edition, Alexandre Dumas. Falsely accused of treason, Edmond Dantès is imprisoned in the bleak Chateau d'If. After a hair-raising escape, he launches an elaborate plot to extract a bitter revenge against those who betrayed him. 448pp. 5‰₆ x 8¼. 0-486-45643-9

CRAFTSMAN BUNGALOWS: Designs from the Pacific Northwest, Yoho & Merritt. This reprint of a rare catalog, showcasing the charming simplicity and cozy style of Craftsman bungalows, is filled with photos of completed homes, plus floor plans and estimated costs. An indispensable resource for architects, historians, and illustrators. 112pp. 10 x 7. 0-486-46875-5

CRAFTSMAN BUNGALOWS: 59 Homes from "The Craftsman," Edited by Gustav Stickley. Best and most attractive designs from Arts and Crafts Movement publication — 1903–1916 — includes sketches, photographs of homes, floor plans, descriptive text. 128pp. 8¼ x 11. 0-486-25829-7

CRIME AND PUNISHMENT, Fyodor Dostoyevsky. Translated by Constance Garnett. Supreme masterpiece tells the story of Raskolnikov, a student tormented by his own thoughts after he murders an old woman. Overwhelmed by guilt and terror, he confesses and goes to prison. 480pp. 5‰₆ x 8¼. 0-486-41587-2

THE DECLARATION OF INDEPENDENCE AND OTHER GREAT DOCUMENTS OF AMERICAN HISTORY: 1775-1865, Edited by John Grafton. Thirteen compelling and influential documents: Henry's "Give Me Liberty or Give Me Death," Declaration of Independence, The Constitution, Washington's First Inaugural Address, The Monroe Doctrine, The Emancipation Proclamation, Gettysburg Address, more. 64pp. 5‰₆ x 8¼. 0-486-41124-9

THE DESERT AND THE SOWN: Travels in Palestine and Syria, Gertrude Bell. "The female Lawrence of Arabia," Gertrude Bell wrote captivating, perceptive accounts of her travels in the Middle East. This intriguing narrative, accompanied by 160 photos, traces her 1905 sojourn in Lebanon, Syria, and Palestine. 368pp. 5⅝ x 8½. 0-486-46876-3

A DOLL'S HOUSE, Henrik Ibsen. Ibsen's best-known play displays his genius for realistic prose drama. An expression of women's rights, the play climaxes when the central character, Nora, rejects a smothering marriage and life in "a doll's house." 80pp. 5‰₆ x 8¼. 0-486-27062-9